T0366817

NATIONS DIVIDED

Georgia Southern University

JACK N. AND ADDIE D. AVERITT LECTURE SERIES

NO. 10

NATIONS DIVIDED

America, Italy, and the
Southern Question

DON H. DOYLE

The University of Georgia Press
Athens & London

© 2002 by the University of Georgia Press
Athens, Georgia 30602
All rights reserved
Designed by Walton Harris
Set in Walbaum
Printed and bound by Maple-Vail

The paper in this book meets the guidelines for
permanence and durability of the Committee on
Production Guidelines for Book Longevity of the
Council on Library Resources.

Printed in the United States of America

02   03   04   05   06   C   5   4   3   2   1

Library of Congress Cataloging-in-Publication Data

Doyle, Don Harrison, 1946–
Nations divided : America, Italy, and the Southern question /
Don H. Doyle.
p.   cm. — (Georgia Southern University. Jack N. and
Addie D. Averitt lecture series ; 10)
Includes bibliographical references and index.
ISBN 0-8203-2330-6 (hardcover : alk. paper)
1. Regionalism—United States—History. 2. Nationalism—United
States—History. 3. United States—Politics and government.
4. Political culture—United States—History. 5. Southern States—History.
6. Regionalism—Italy—History. 7. Nationalism—Italy—History.
8. Italy—Politics and government. 9. Political culture—Italy—History.
10. Italy, Southern—History. I. Title.
II. Jack N. and Addie D. Averitt lecture series ; no. 10.
E179.5 .D74 2002
320.54'0973—dc21   2002000862

British Library Cataloging-in-Publication Data available

*per Marjorie
e la nostra vita nuova*

CONTENTS

FOREWORD

On October 19 and 20, 2000, Georgia Southern University celebrated the tenth anniversary of the Jack N. and Addie D. Averitt
Lecture Series. The speaker was Don H. Doyle, who holds the
Nelson Tyrone Jr. Chair in History at Vanderbilt University. He
approached the series' theme, "Regions and Identities," from an
international perspective and cast new light on the role of regionalism, along with other factors, in national unification and civil war.
How can people overcome fundamental differences such as region,
race, ethnicity, religion, and language to form one nation? What
happens when political unity disintegrates and parochial loyalties
pull a nation apart? These are the questions that Professor Doyle
explored in his lectures and that he examines in greater depth in
the essays in this volume.

Doyle's comparison of the United States and Italy demonstrates
that nationalism is a powerful agent that shapes identity and in-
spires individuals to sacrifice their own interests—and sometimes
their lives—for a common cause. Nationalism, he argues, is not
a vague abstraction created and propagated by political and cultural elites. It is, instead, a dynamic force that draws its meaning
and vigor from the ideas and actions of ordinary citizens. Doyle
delineates nationalism as it is incorporated into popular culture
and practiced in daily life. Civilians and soldiers who participated
in pageants and parades; townspeople who raised money to build
monuments and memorials; teachers who passed patriotic lore and
legend on to their students—all had a hand in constructing na-

tional identity. If nationalism is a civil religion, as some scholars have argued, Doyle establishes that it is characterized by a pattern of call and response rather than by liturgical commandments issued from on high.

National solidarity is often forged through vilification of a real or imagined enemy and, as Doyle's analysis of the "southern question" in the United States and Italy shows, sometimes that enemy can come from within. Regionalism—"southernness"—became the counterweight by which national values were measured. For northerners in both countries, southerners served as foils for models of civic virtue, rebels who refused to conform to national ideals. Southern Italians and white southerners in the United States resented attempts to obliterate their customs and institutions in the name of nationalism. In both places, the North and its vision of national unity prevailed, but regionalism persisted as southerners created their own myths of nations lost.

Despite the differences between the historical experiences of the United States and Italy, these essays reveal that the two nations—and the two Souths that have so often been at odds with their northern compatriots—share much in common. The comparison provides some useful lessons. Americans bewildered by civil wars in countries around the globe would do well to remember the bitter strife in their own history. At the same time, as Doyle eloquently argues, the American struggle to build and sustain a heterogeneous nation "may offer some insights, even hope, for a world of nations undergoing turmoil brought about by migration, ethnic conflict, and separatist rebellion."

Many people have contributed to the success of the Averitt Lecture Series. Past and present administrators at Georgia Southern, including President Bruce Grube, Provost Vaughn Vandegrift, Interim Dean of the College of Liberal Arts and Social Sciences Jeffrey

Buller, and History Department Chair Jerome O. Steffen, have recognized the importance of the series to the university and the community. Wesley Sumner of the public relations office assisted with publicity, and graduate students from the History Department served as ushers during the lectures. Malcolm Call and Alison Waldenberg of the University of Georgia Press have made the publication process a pleasure and have offered valuable advice as well. Alan C. Downs, co-chair of the History Department's Averitt Lecture Series Committee, and committee members Ruth A. Thompson and Jeffrey R. Young cheerfully fulfilled their responsibilities. History Department secretaries Patricia Lanier and Lisa Sapp deserve special thanks for handling countless details with their customary serenity, efficiency, and patience.

The lecture series is made possible by a gift from Jack N. and Addie D. Averitt. Professor Doyle's topic was of particular interest to Mrs. Averitt, who maintained a lifelong commitment to helping people understand and overcome the differences that spawn hatred among individuals and war among nations. Unfortunately, for the first time since the series was inaugurated in 1990, she was unable to accompany Dr. Averitt to the lectures. Two months later, on December 19, 2000, she passed away. A native of Tennessee, Mrs. Averitt was a graduate of Peabody College in Nashville. She moved to Statesboro in 1946 to accept a position as reference librarian at Georgia Teachers' College, now Georgia Southern University. From that time onward she played an active role in academic and civic life on campus, in the community, and in the region. She promoted the cultural enrichment of students, faculty, and local residents, and fostered understanding among people of diverse backgrounds. Long before globalism became a watchword in higher education, Rotary International honored her for "her selfless work expanding human horizons to encompass the globe." She became the first woman to receive the organization's Distinguished Service Award.

Possessing dignity, grace, and a generous spirit, she had the unerring ability to put everyone she met at ease. Her death was a great loss to her family, her friends, and the community, but her memory and the values she cherished will endure in the lecture series that bears her name.

ANASTATIA SIMS

Co-chair, Averitt Lecture Series Committee

PREFACE

This book deals with the two most important features of American history: the creation of a new nation and the secessionist rebellion that tore it apart. The American Revolution and the American Civil War define one nation's special history, but they also have meaning to the world of nations that has taken form since the late eighteenth century. This book invites readers to look at America's experience in the broader context of that international world and see it as one of many stories about building nations that contain diverse peoples and interests.

One of the more exciting areas of scholarly inquiries in recent years has been the study of nationalism, particularly its historical origins. It is a subject that demands conversation across academic and political frontiers and bears on the most salient issues of our present time as well as our past. But in reading the theoretical and case study literature on nationalism I was struck by how the United States, and the Americas in general, have been ignored in this discussion, even when American scholars have been major contributors to it. In two collections of essays designed to introduce readers to the scholarship on nationalism (*Becoming National: A Reader*, edited by Geoff Eley and Ronald Grigor Suny [1996], and *Nationalism*, edited by John Hutchinson and Anthony D. Smith [1994]), not one of the dozens of articles and book excerpts focuses on the United States and only a few even mention it. Except for one piece on Latin America, it would seem the entire Western Hemisphere has been left out of the current discussion of nationalism.

This book is a modest effort toward correcting this omission and, I hope, a stimulus to others. The United States is significant not only because it was the "first new nation" but also because it serves as a prime example of "civic nationalism." Whereas ethnic nationalism rests on the idea of common descent, religion, language, or other deeply rooted primordial traits, civic nationalism is a political concept that defines the nation as a common government, a state that may encompass a variety of ethnic and cultural groups. It is a nationalism based on common belief, not blood.

One essential challenge to American nationhood has been the problem of defining a community out of a remarkable diversity of immigrants, religions, and cultures. Another has been its regional diversity, most conspicuously the conflicted relationship between the South and the rest of the nation, which resulted in a separatist rebellion, a bloody Civil War, a frustrated Reconstruction, and a legacy of tension. The American experience of cultural diversity and regional conflict, I believe, is increasingly relevant to many nations facing massive migration from without and regional conflict from within. How nations define themselves and their membership is of supreme importance to our ability to live together, to imagine a community capable of embracing diverse citizens.

Instead of casting the American example into an amorphous transnational study, I have chosen instead to begin working within a more manageable framework that compares the United States with one European counterpart, Italy. This focus allows us to see the parallel and contrasting experiences of two nations that, despite obvious differences, shared common problems in defining nationhood. The making of Italy, like that of the United States, involved the amalgamation of many diverse cultural groups. Also like the United States, Italy confronted a South (an ill-defined area the Italians call the *Mezzogiorno*) that seemed at odds with the ideals of the new nation, at least as those ideals came to be defined by northerners.

This book is based on lectures I gave at Georgia Southern University in October 2000, in the Jack N. and Addie D. Averitt Lecture Series. I am very grateful to the Averitts for their generous support of this event. Dr. Jack N. Averitt attended the lectures and hosted a wonderful dinner for me during my visit. Mrs. Averitt was ill at that time, and I was saddened to learn later of her death. Thanks also to the Department of History at Georgia Southern and its Averitt Lectures committee—Alan Downs, Anastatia Sims, Ruth A. Thompson, and Jeffrey R. Young—for inviting me. I am especially grateful to Anastatia Sims for her wonderful hospitality during our tour of Statesboro and Savannah.

Most of the research and writing took place during a sabbatical year in 1999–2000. I feel very fortunate to be at a university that recognizes the importance of research and supports it generously. Thanks to Vanderbilt University's College of Arts and Sciences for granting me leave and to the University Research Council for a travel grant. During the fall of 1999 I enjoyed affiliation with the Institute for Historical Research in London. While there I attended the seminar in Modern Italian History and enjoyed stimulating conversations with Lucy Riall, John Dickie, Rick Halpern, and many others. I found in the new British Library a wealth of published materials on the history of Italy and a delightful place to work. During the spring of 2000 I enjoyed a pleasant and fruitful month of study at the American Academy in Rome, where I had begun my love affair with Italy some nine years earlier. Later that spring I was a fellow at the Liguria Study Center for the Arts and Humanities in Bogliasco, Italy. Surrounded by the beauty of the Italian Riviera, a group of fascinating fellows, and many good friends in Genoa, I managed nonetheless to make my Bogliasco stay extraordinarily fruitful. I am very grateful to the staff of the center and to the Bogliasco Foundation for making that possible.

Many others generously expedited my journey into the field of Italian history. Marta Petruvesic has been of extraordinary help to me from the outset. Alberto Banti shared his bibliography and his wisdom. The Italian Fulbright Commission sponsored two memorable experiences as a Fulbright Professor in Rome and Genoa. I am especially grateful to Larry Gray and Luigi Filadoro of the commission, and to the USIA in Rome for their support of an international conference held in Naples in June 1997, "The Southern Question: Nationalism and Regionalism in Italy and America." Franco Benigno, Director of IMES (Istituto Meridionale di Storia e Scienze Sociali), the leading force for southern studies in Italy, cosponsored the event. It was the stimulating exchange that took place at the conference that started me contemplating the present book. I am grateful to all those who participated in that event and especially to all those I have failed to name who aided me in my struggle to better understand the history of these two nations.

Sue Marasco, Peter Kruyla, Adrienne Lerner, Lee Ann Reynolds, and Henry Davenport, students in my graduate seminar on nationalism, offered helpful comments on an earlier draft of this book. Ed Harcourt cast his keen eye over an earlier version of this manuscript and saved me from numerous errors. Thanks to Lucy Riall, who made several useful suggestions. I am grateful to Alison Waldenberg of the University of Georgia Press for all she has done to bring this book to life. The copyeditor, Trudie Calvert, straightened out my untidy writing with unusual skill. With great sadness I learned later that she did her work from a hospice; it was one of her last completed jobs.

Dozens of people who participate in the discussion groups on H-Net dealing with Italian and United States history have taken time to answer my queries. I am especially grateful to those in Italian history who very kindly helped a novice understand some of the intricacies of their field. The internet nation is an imagined community whose members I may never know except through cyberspace, but it has been a community of very real benefit to me in my research and writing.

This book is dedicated to Marjorie Spruill, who came into my life fortuitously just as I was finishing the last revisions. She shares with me a love of the past and hope for the future—the essence of new unions both imagined and real.

NATIONS DIVIDED

1

A Death at Gettysburg

During a research trip to Mississippi some years ago I came across a collection of papers and letters between Jeremiah Gage, a student at the University of Mississippi from 1857 to 1861, and his parents in Holmes County. His early letters were filled with much the same thoughts that young men today write in letters (or e-mails) when they are away from home for the first time. He wrote of the young ladies he was meeting in Oxford and admonished his little sister back home to stay away from men whose reputation he thought questionable. Among the letters I also found evidence of some intellectual stirrings in this young man. An essay written in 1858 was on the meaning of Christopher Columbus to America. During a summer trip to the archives one of the last things I wanted to do was read another undergraduate essay, but this one caught my attention for its remarkable patriotic zeal:

> Among the many geniuses, whose names have been heralded abroad and praised by posterity, there is no one who deserves greater praise than intrepid Columbus. . . . The greatness of his mind taught him that there was still a favored land, lashed by the foaming waves of the Atlantic, rich in soil and in mines; where, uninterrupted by the clanking chains of despotism, posterity might live and enjoy freedom of speech and worship God as they

might wish. This being his great object, he with great endurance and undaunted courage was led by the hand of God to behold the land of America, spreading forth its beauty, loveliness, and richness; inviting the heroic navigator to rest within its lovely confines. Yes, it was by his great genius, that our fore-fathers were released from servitude; and were led to behold a land untrodden by base and corrupted tyrants. By his unparalleled exertions, he has shed a light of burning glory upon the face of the globe; which will never cease to shine with brilliancy, and increase in splendor, as long as the name of Columbus is engraved on the hearts of the American people.[1]

Like most of the students at the University of Mississippi, Jerry Gage was the son of a wealthy planter. Though his family owned many slaves, he saw no contradiction in praising Columbus for discovering a land where the "American people" could be "released from servitude." Nor did he seem aware of Columbus's own endeavor to enslave the inhabitants he found in the New World. Gage graduated with the class of 1860 and stayed on to take a degree in law in 1861. That spring all thoughts of academics were overshadowed by the secession crisis. Mississippi had followed South Carolina out of the Union in January, and across the land people were preparing for war. Some of the more militant students defied the administration's orders by forming a military company and conducting drills on campus. Jerry Gage was among those who enlisted with the University Greys in April 1861 and went off to fight in Virginia for the Confederate States of America. He was severely wounded at the Battle of Gaines' Mill but recovered to fight at Gettysburg in early July 1863. The boys of the University Greys were in the front ranks of George Pickett's charge on the third day of battle.

William Faulkner wrote of that afternoon when the South might have succeeded in its struggle to become a nation, an empire even.

This was the day, he wrote, that "every Southern boy fourteen years old" can recall, that "instant when it's still not yet two oclock on that July afternoon in 1863, the brigades are in position behind the rail fence, the guns are laid and ready in the woods and the furled flags are already loosened to break out and Pickett . . . looking up the hill waiting for Longstreet to give the word and it's all in the balance, it hasn't happened yet." There they stood, on the brink of triumph, or failure, "with all this much to lose and all this much to gain: Pennsylvania, Maryland, the world, the golden dome of Washington itself to crown with desperate and unbelievable victory." When it finally "happened," of course, the dream of an independent South died at Gettysburg and—on the same day across the would-be nation—in Vicksburg.

Jerry Gage was also about to die as he lay on his cot in a battlefield hospital. He had been among the first to fall that afternoon. Half of the former students in the University Greys were killed before it was over; the other half were wounded. A cannonball had nearly ripped his left arm off below the elbow, tore into his abdomen, and took away much of his left side. They were about to give him morphine when a hospital aide asked if he wanted to say goodbye to anyone. He lived long enough to pen a farewell letter to his mother back in Mississippi.

Gettysburg, Penn. July 3rd.

My Dear Mother.

This is the last you may ever hear from me. I have time to tell you that I died like a man. Bear my loss as best you can. Remember that I am true to my country and my greatest regret at dying is that she is not free and that you and my sisters are robbed of my worth whatever that may be. I hope this will reach you and you must not regret that my body can not be obtained. It is a mere matter of form anyhow.

This is for my sisters too as I can not write more. Send my
dying release to Miss Mary . . . you know who.

> J. S. Gage
> Co. "A" 11th Miss.

At the bottom of the letter he wrote: "This letter is stained with
my blood."[2]

This young man who had written so earnestly about Columbus
and the American people three years earlier gave his life for what
he called "my country," the Confederate States of America, a nation
born in rebellion *against* the United States of America. He obviously
felt powerful loyalties and affection for his parents and family and
to Mary (his sweetheart back home). But it was to this nation that
he gave his life on a battlefield hundreds of miles from these loved
ones. His letter implies that his mother and family fully shared his
values and that they would be proud that he "died like a man" for
the country they shared. Inheritors of a twentieth-century world in
which sacrifice for one's country is taken for granted may not find
this so strange. But it had not always been so and may not always be
so in the future. To ask what excited such fervent loyalty and deadly
sacrifice in Jerry Gage—or the soldier who killed him—is to ask
how that world with its intense national loyalties took hold.

REBELS INTERNATIONAL

The seed for this book, I now realize, was planted more than thirty
years ago in graduate school at Northwestern University, where
my mentor, George Fredrickson, introduced me to comparative
history. But that seed did not begin to sprout until exposed to the
warm Italian sun a few years ago. I had been invited to Genoa in
1995 to serve as Fulbright Professor of American History, and I
found myself teaching Italian students the history of America as
a foreign country. I suppose it is like teaching English as a foreign

language, when one sees familiar idiomatic expressions and words in a strange new light. As a historian of America teaching in Italy I began to see many taken-for-granted features of my country's history as puzzling and problematic once they needed to be explained to those who did not take them for granted. I also began to see parallels and contrasts that made me think in new ways about our separate pasts.

During my stay in Italy what Italians call the "Southern Question" had emerged once again as a subject of debate. A political movement in the North, the Lega Nord or Northern League, had gained notoriety by denouncing the South and calling for secession from Italy. I remember while driving around Lake Como seeing road signs with stickers that proclaimed "La Republica del Nord Italia."

As I taught American history, read Italian history, and talked with Italian professors and students that spring, it was difficult *not* to think comparatively. While visiting Sicily and Naples an American could not help but notice the presence of a distinctive symbol, the Confederate battle flag. This familiar and disconcerting image could be seen on bumper stickers and, I was told, on flags that Neapolitan fans waved at soccer games. For them, it was a symbol of southern pride if not rebellion.

"Do southerners in Italy know what this flag means?" I asked an Italian professor of American literature over lunch in Naples one day. "Oh, yes, we know what it means," she answered readily. "We too are a defeated people. Once we were a rich and independent country, and then they came from the North and conquered us and took our wealth and power away to Rome."[3] My Neapolitan friend and those waving the Confederate flag at soccer matches were engaged in their own style of comparative history—it got me thinking.

Before coming to Italy, I had been part of a faculty seminar at Vanderbilt that discussed "the South as an American Problem"; a book of our essays came out later that year.[4] As I learned more about "the South as an Italian Problem" I realized that whatever their many differences, each nation had within it a region that came to represent the "other Italy" and the "other America." Against the image of this internal "other" both nations had defined themselves much as they had in conflicts with foreign nations.[5] Paradoxically, opposition within nations could produce cohesion.

It could also produce conflict, often to the point that separation seemed the only answer. During the 1990s it seemed that separatism, or some form of regional rebellion against national governments, had become the order of the day. To America's north, French-speaking citizens of Quebec were calling for separation and independence from Canada. To the south, the Zapatistas were seizing local power in southern Mexico, rebelling against the Mexican government, and protesting the effects of globalization on their lives. In Asia and Africa, the main expressions of nationalism and separatism have come in a series of colonial uprisings against European rule. These colonial revolts have required a continual redrawing of maps since World War II. No sooner have some new postcolonial nations established their independence than they have faced separatist revolts from within. From Pakistan and Sri Lanka to East Timor and Eritrea, separatism has brought nationalism full circle by fomenting internal revolts against the very nations that themselves had been formed in rebellion against colonial rule. Americans—especially southerners—can fully appreciate this irony.

In Europe, meanwhile, the word "former" came to be attached to Yugoslavia, the Soviet Union, and Czechoslovakia. In Yugoslavia, vicious wars erupted between Serbs and Croats, then between Serbs and Kosovors, peoples who had once lived together more or less peacefully. These civil wars combined ethnic, religious, and territorial conflict and brought the chilling term "ethnic cleansing" into our daily vocabulary. Across the former Soviet Union, the world witnessed the separatist impulse play out in several places that broke away from the USSR. Within the Russian Federation itself, secessionist movements challenged Russian hegemony, nowhere more violently than in Chechnya. Meanwhile, in Western Europe the Irish, Scottish, Basque, and Corsican independence movements continued as seasoned veterans of the separatist struggle.[6]

In Britain the Scottish independence movement found new life in the 1990s inspired to no small degree by the Hollywood film on William Wallace, *Braveheart*. In 1997 Scottish voters marked the seven hundredth anniversary of Wallace's victory at Stirling Bridge with a landslide vote in favor of restoring the parliament in Edinburgh that had been abolished since the union with England in 1707. The Welsh independence movement had gained intensity during the 1970s, at times with violent anti-English strains. It re-emerged during the 1990s but with less success than its Scottish counterpart, for in Wales the 1997 referendum on home rule met crushing defeat. Nonetheless, "devolution," as the British call it, came in bloodless concessions of increased regional autonomy. What Tom Nairn calls the "break-up of Britain" seemed to be the final phase in the collapse of the British Empire. It reversed the expansion that began centuries earlier with the movement of Greater England to dominate the outer reaches of Great Britain, then Ireland, then North America.[7] Across the Irish Sea, in Northern Ireland the "troubles" between the English rulers and Irish people had a long and bloody history of exactly the kind the United Kingdom hoped to avoid with devolution. Whether such a fierce separatist rebellion was ever likely in Scotland or Wales, the willingness of Scots and Welsh citizens to identify with their own "people" as opposed to being "British" was sufficient to warrant a measure of separation. Each phase of devolution left the so-called United Kingdom a little less united.

Meanwhile, in 1996 Italy's Lega Nord declared its own nation, called "Padania," referring vaguely to the area surrounding the

Po River valley. Without firing a shot this pseudonation issued its declaration of independence with a familiar prelude: "When in the course of human events it becomes necessary for one Peoples [*sic*] to dissolve the bands which bind them with another." Padania wrote a "provisional" constitution, formed a separate parliament, minted its own money, published a newspaper, set up radio and television stations, flew its own flag, and organized a web site. Perhaps most portentous, this nation began its own beauty pageant acclaiming "Miss Padania." All it lacked was a football team.[8]

Subnational conflict within nations became as powerful a force in the latter part of the twentieth century as national independence and unification were in the nineteenth century. Consequently, the world of nations has proliferated in numbers. Fifty nations signed the United Nations charter in 1945; there were 188 members at the end of the century, many of them postcolonial states; others were born of separatist movements against other member nations.[9]

In recent times the media are filled with talk of the coming "postnational" era in which the globalization of the economy, the communications revolution, the spread of English as a world language, and widespread migration will render national boundaries irrelevant. It seems at times that we are converging into one world, one language, one economy, and one community of people living together in a "United Nations of the World." Yet a powerful undertow of nationalism and separatism within nations continues to rage against this global blurring of lines. It is as though these "mixed marriages" we call nations, which began with such passion, hope, and affection, have run afoul over irreconcilable differences and wind up in ugly divorces and nasty custody battles. "Separatism is a fact," the journalist Charles Krauthammer wrote in 1995, "the single greatest political fact of the post–cold war world. With external enemies removed, with hybrid states no longer held together by hegemonic superpowers, the petty annoyances and existential difficulties of living in mixed-ethnic marriages within nation states has become intolerable." Movements for separation, he warned, "are a herald of the death of diversity. They are a living refutation of the warm and cozy notion, based more on hope than on history, of multicultural harmony and strength."[10]

Those witnessing the history of the United States had issued equally dire warnings, some with alarm, others with smug satisfaction. For many conservatives (in Britain especially) the Civil War proved that the American experiment in democracy and diversity could not survive in so vast a nation. James Spence, a Liverpool merchant, felt certain that the American experiment in democracy would lead to "national decadence" and the "increasing inferiority of the race" and that a nation with such "great differences of manners, habits, and customs" could never survive as one nation.[11]

Indeed, internal conflict has been rife throughout the history of the United States. There have been intense, often violent, clashes among racial and ethnic groups: Irish Catholics battling Protestants over what would be taught in public schools or whether saloons would be closed on Sundays; African Americans and whites battling over urban turf or access to public facilities. Except for the 1860s, however, these internal conflicts have rarely taken on the territorial dimension necessary to support genuine separatist movements. A recurring strain of black nationalism has sought different forms of territorial separatism in back-to-Africa movements or in "Exodusters" who migrated to Kansas, for example. Generally, however, black nationalism has encouraged cultural autonomy rather than territorial separatism. Aggrieved minorities in America may denounce assimilation, but they rarely pursue genuine separatism as a viable remedy.

For all its troubled history of internal strife, the United States has endured as a nation and one that tolerates a remarkable range of diverse peoples. It is a history that may offer some insights, even hope, for a world of nations undergoing turmoil brought by migration, ethnic conflict, and separatist rebellion. By viewing their own past in the light of recent events, Americans might also better understand other countries undergoing their own travails of nationhood. Americans like to think of themselves as being innocent of the vicious ethnic warfare that has raged in the Old World and over so much of the globe. Europeans, in turn, enjoy reminding Americans of how little history they have (New World history beginning, in this view, only after the Europeans show up). Both views obscure the common ground on which nations in the New and Old Worlds were built in the modern era and the parallel struggle to accommodate the diverse peoples who inhabit those nations.

The United States is not so young and innocent; in fact, it is the oldest among modern democratic nations. Not only is it the "first new nation" born in colonial revolt against the central government, the United States was also among the first to experience a massive separatist rebellion.[12] What might well have become the "former United States of America" became in the late 1860s a scarred and grizzled veteran of nationalism and its discontents. The revolutionary origins of America, its history of civil war and reconciliation, offer many examples—often unhappy ones—of the challenge of making nations out of diverse peoples and the terrible cost of failure. For many nations of the world the American past would become their future.

ization, the necessary invention of an egalitarian industrial society that repudiated the inherited hierarchies of traditional society. Gellner's modern nations, at least those European nations he is most familiar with, justify their existence on the mythology of a homogeneous ethnic kinship and a continuous past.[5]

These are only some of the more notable scholars who have shaped the current understanding of nationalism and national identity as something constructed and invented rather than natural, primordial, and continuous. Modern nations, they tell us, are recent, artificial, and, by implication, temporary. Like Adam, as Gellner puts it, modern nations are born "without navels," and the task of nationalists is to invent those navels, to explain their origin. This approach to nationalism and national identity as something that is invented complements the new idiom of postmodern thinking with its emphasis on the constructed nature of culture and its opposition to notions of essentiality.

If primordialism has been debunked in academic circles, it remains a powerful source of identity among many peoples of the world, as more than one scholar has reminded us. Clifford Geertz, an anthropologist who studies postcolonial societies in Asia, distinguishes between primordial and civic ties as two rival sources of popular identity. When strong primordial identities, among religious fundamentalists or ethnic minorities for example, coexist with modern secular identities, they can produce great conflict, the resolution of which may involve separatism or repression.[6] Anthony Smith, one of the leading theorists of nationalism, tells us that beneath the imagined identities constructed by nationalist ideology there are often deeply embedded and very real ethnic and religious roots. "Nations and nationalisms" are constructed, he tells us, but often they "are also the products of pre-existing traditions and heritages which have coalesced over the generations."[7]

While within the groves of academe scholars busy themselves with the deconstruction of "imagined communities" and "invented traditions," the fires of ethnic and religious nationalism continue to rage around the world. People fight and die and sacrifice in countless ways for what they perceive to be their national identity, and they inflict terrible suffering and devastation on others in the cause of national sovereignty or ethnic purity. I sometimes imagine one of today's postmodern scholars impaled on the bayonet of some fanatical nationalist, blood gushing from his mouth, explaining: "You realize that this nation you are fighting for is nothing more than an artificial cultural construct."

Not long after I imagined this fanciful encounter I learned of a conflict between academic skepticism and zealous primordial nationalism that was all too real. Ronald Grigor Suny, a leading scholar of nationalism and a specialist on Soviet Russia and Armenia, was invited to a conference in Armenia in 1997, not long after the Republic of Armenia had become independent of the Soviet Union. The thrust of his talk, he explained, "was to question the usefulness of ethno-nationalism in the current situation by proposing a more constructivist understanding of nationness in place of the primordialist convictions of the nationalist." Nations, he told his Armenian audience, "are congealed histories . . . made up of stories that people tell about their past and thereby determine who they are." "Whatever actually happened is far less important than how it is remembered," he explained, and went on to show how particular atrocities suffered by Armenians in the past had been distorted to serve the nationalist cause. Professor Suny's talk met with hostile questions and angry denunciations, some questioning his Armenian ethnicity, others accusing him of loyalty to Russia. He was surrounded by an angry crowd and had to be escorted from the room by security guards. Leaflets were distributed the next day attacking his talk, and a year later a book appeared denouncing his work along with that of others who questioned the nationalist history of Armenia.[8] Academic skepticism about the constructed nature of the "imagined community" ran head-on into a very real community of believers.

Contemporary scholarship on nationalism has effectively demolished the idea that nations derive from authentic primordial ties of blood and tradition. What it has not done so well is to help us understand why so many people embrace these national identities with such zeal and how such identities take form. Nor does it explain some very powerful forms of nationalism in countries like the United States and in Latin American nations where there was no pretense of ethnic kinship and historical continuity.

The idea among scholars that modern nationalism is rooted in some primordial identity is itself an intellectual construction, and it distorts the actual history of nationalism as it evolved in the Americas and Western Europe. The celebration of the nation as a new idea and a repudiation of the past was, of course, central to the founding of the United States and most Latin American republics. But it was also fundamental to the liberal nationalism of Europe that came out of the Enlightenment. European nationalists such as Giuseppe Mazzini embraced the modern nation as an ideal that could unite and inspire people who may not belong to a community bound by blood. This idealist basis for nationhood was also fundamental to the French Revolution, which gave birth to a powerful revolutionary ideology that transcended political boundaries to assault the Old Regime. To be sure, many European nationalists also embraced a primordialist justification for their claim to exist as a nation. The German nationalist Johann Gottfried Herder envisioned the German nation as an organic entity based on essential affinities of blood, language, and culture. But this brand of primordialist nationalism was not the dominant mode, and it often coexisted with liberal ideals of nationalism and progress that transcended the past.[9]

Much of the current scholarship on nationalism is colored by reaction to the horrors nationalism has visited on the twentieth century. In place of the liberal humanitarian ideals of equality, liberty, and progress that inspired early nationalism, in the twentieth century nationalism is more often associated with war, imperialism, racism, and genocide. The underlying implication in much of the current scholarship is that nationalism is not only a false god but an evil one as well. There is no denying that nationalism has been a tool put to bad purposes, but it is important that we not conflate all expressions of nationalism with its most hideous twentieth-century examples. For now, let us revisit the first century of liberal nationalism when it was a new, revolutionary force, one capable of imagining and realizing new communities of diverse peoples based on liberty, equality, and the pursuit of happiness.[10]

INVENTING AMERICA

Viewed within the traditional European paradigm that defines a nation as a distinctive people, place, and past, the United States hardly qualifies. Walker Conner contrasts the United States against the European standard for nationhood: "Whatever the American people are (and they may well be *sui generis*), they are not a nation in the pristine sense of the word." The "unfortunate habit" of referring to the United States as a nation and thus "equating American with German, Chinese, English," he tells us, "has seduced scholars into erroneous analogies." The "absence of a common origin," Conner goes on, makes it difficult, "conceivably impossible, for the American to appreciate instinctively the idea of the nation," to "appreciate what it means for a German to be German."[11]

Conner's confining usage of the term "nation" treats the American model as the aberrant exception, but we may want to reconsider just how unusual this standard for nationhood has been in the modern world. Though it may lack the ethnic and historical roots many Europeans presume to be necessary for nationhood, the

United States became an important prototype for nations of the Americas and Europe, as well as non-Western nations. The American model defined the sources of nationhood in political rather than ethnic terms, in belief rather than blood, but these served nonetheless as sturdy foundations for national identity and purpose. Benedict Anderson treats the American republics as "Creole pioneers" in the age of nationalism. "Not only were they historically the first such states to emerge on the world stage," he writes, but they "provided the first real models of what such states should 'look like.'"[12] Instead of understanding the United States as a sui generis nation, we may see it as part of a larger transatlantic enterprise that spawned a variety of national types. Some found legitimacy in the claim that they shared common blood and a long, continuous history. Others, like the United States, instead came into existence claiming neither a distinctive people nor much of a past. In the United States nationalism was born in colonial rebellion against the mother country, a nation with whom it had strong ties of blood and history.

Until quite late in the conflict between Britain and its North American colonies, the differences at issue might easily have been resolved without even the threat of independence as a remedy. There were few signs of a rising tide of American nationalism before 1775, nor was there any strong sense on either side of the Atlantic of a separate American people. The American cause began as protest against British policy, not against the legitimacy of British rule or the British as a people. Following a century and more of development under the light hand of British colonial rule, several new regulations affecting trade, settlement, taxation, and finance were introduced at the end of the French and Indian War in 1763. A growing number of colonists thought these new measures to be harmful to colonial interests and unjustly imposed. By no means, however, were these obnoxious new policies understood by any but the most radical extremists to be justification for revolution or something to be remedied by separation from Britain—not at first anyway. The "long train of abuses," as Thomas Jefferson referred to them, ensuing between the Stamp Act in 1765 and the first shots fired at Lexington and Concord ten years later all centered on the American effort to reverse British policy and restore the colonial status quo. The failure of colonial protests finally led to a reluctant break with Britain.[13]

British policies were interpreted for the colonists by ideologues like Tom Paine who read the events not simply as bad policy produced by misdirected or malevolent men in government but as indications of an evil system that Americans must escape. In its origins it was clear that American nationalism rested on political principles, not on any claim that Americans were a distinctive people.

Most striking about the American experience in nation building is how sparse and frail the building materials were. It is difficult to imagine a new country less endowed with what are traditionally thought to be the essential ingredients for nationhood. If a nation is a people who occupy a common territory and share some elements of national cohesion (common language, ethnicity, religion, customs, or history), then the British colonies in North America simply failed to qualify on almost every count. Indeed, even the name of the new nation, the United States of America, betrayed a lack of a clear, coherent identity, and the appropriation of "America" as a moniker did little to overcome that.

Americans wishing to invent nationhood out of a shared past had little to work with. They had, for the most part, consciously rejected the culture of the native peoples, and whatever history and tradition most European Americans could claim was that of English colonists. To reject their British past, and with it their British identity, was to discard one of the very few things that might unite the colonists in North America. Britain gave most of the colonists their language, their religion, their system of law, and many of the ideas they now employed to voice their grievances.[14]

Americans might have emphasized their non-Englishness. Aside from the large numbers of natives and African slaves, at the time of the Revolution historians estimate that 40 percent of whites in the thirteen colonies were non-English in origin. In Pennsylvania and New York, with their huge influxes of Scots-Irish, Germans, and Dutch, those of English origin were less than a quarter of the population. In New England, where whites were overwhelmingly English ethnically, there had been very little in-migration since the English Civil War in the 1640s, which meant that most were American born and had been for several generations by the 1770s. Instead of rebelling against an alien oppressor with no right to rule them, Americans began from the very opposite premise, that "we are one of you" and deserve to be treated equally as "freeborn Englishmen."

American identity could nest comfortably within British identity so long as colonists had no cause to feel excluded or inferior. But these nested identities of British and American began to grate as the interests and sentiments that bound them broke down. The friction between British and American identities, the historian Timothy Breen argues, was the result not of a growing sense of American separateness but of the rise of *British* nationalism in the later part of the eighteenth century. The triumph of British military prowess and imperial success left many American subjects on the fringes of the empire feeling they no longer fully belonged. Especially during and after the French and Indian War, British nationalism sharpened the sense of difference between England and its American colonies on both sides of the Atlantic and nearly always to the debasement of America.[15]

Building a nation out of so diverse and volatile a people as inhabited the American colonies would require more than shared grievances against haughty rulers. Many feared that without British identity the colonists would quickly shatter into a contentious set of hostile settlements. John Dickinson of Pennsylvania worried that independence would bring nothing more than "A Multitude of Commonwealths, Crimes, and Calamities, of mutual Jealousies, Hatreds, Wars and Devastations; till at last the exhausted Provinces shall sink into Slavery under the yoke of some fortunate Conqueror."[16] That the Revolution did not dissolve quickly into this anticipated mess of jealousies and hatreds was in no small part the result of the imminent challenge of mounting a war for independence, fashioning an alliance among thirteen contentious colonies, and giving people good reasons to fight and support a risky revolt for independence. In their violent beginnings in wars for independence, young nations such as the United States not only invented justification for becoming a nation, they also found powerful motives to unite against the enemy—or die trying.

American nationalism, such as it was, emerged within an independence movement in search of an ideology. The revolutionary liberalism that sprang out of this colonial rebellion, Breen argues, was an effective "rhetorical strategy" that served as "the political language of a colonial people who had not yet invented a nation" and had no "common history." It was, Breen asserts, the rebellion against a "newly aggressive English state" that eventually "forced the Americans to leap out of history and to defend colonial and human equality on the basis of timeless natural rights."[17] American revolutionaries advanced timeless principles and natural rights, but American nationalists dared not make their case for separation on any timeless and natural affinities or on any essential differences with Britain. The case for nationhood could never rest on such primordialist claims.

American nationalism had to be invented, and quickly, in the maelstrom of war. Beginning in the 1760s, the historian Jack Greene argues, British Americans who before had apologized for the inferiority of their culture, now in the midst of revolution "defined more fully than ever before what made their societies both different from those of the Old World and similar to each other."

Greene goes on to state that in "the process of thus elaborating their Americanness, they quickly began to develop an infinitely more favorable sense of collective self." We can see this before the Revolution during nonimportation protests against British tax policy when Americans redefined such imports as British clothing as "effeminate" and "aristocratic" while American homespun was to be worn with patriotic pride. In consumption and in manners America's rustic simplicity came to be praised as a virtue in contrast to British aristocratic decadence.

Out of this forced self-justification, Greene tells us, "American observers more and more began to entertain the possibility that their country might have a distinctive role to play in the course of human affairs." They anticipated the day when America would, in the words of one unidentified enthusiast, "be the glory and the astonishment of the whole earth" and when the very "name of AMERICAN," would "carry honour and majesty in the sound—and men [would] esteem it a blessing to wear [that] venerable and commanding stile." Informed by revolutionary propagandists such as Tom Paine, Americans began to realize they had things to teach Europe. America would become the "laboratory for Enlightenment ideas" and a "workshop for liberty." The Revolution, Timothy Dwight announced, had introduced a new era, and "the rest of the world" would "follow the laudable example of America."[18] American nationalism would derive its inspiration not from an imagined past of common experience that had spawned a people but instead from an imagined future whose promise lay in transcending the past.

By the side of the Old North Bridge in Concord, where Americans first confronted His Majesty's troops in armed rebellion, are the graves of the British soldiers killed on April 19, 1775. On a stone marking the burial site are the poignant words of the poet James Russell Lowell, which summarize the American interpretation of what the British were about that day: "They came three thousand miles and died / To keep the past upon its throne." On what we may call the American side of the bridge stands a bronze statue of the citizen soldier, holding a musket and plow, with the famous inscription by Ralph Waldo Emerson: "Here once the embattled farmers stood, / And fired the shot heard round the world." This was a revolution of the future against the past, but only in retrospect, for even as they fired on His Majesty's troops, the Minutemen were protesting the changing world the British had upset. They wanted to *restore* liberty and just rule; the revolution they started hurled them into the future.[19]

Instead of drawing on the past, American nationalism of necessity had to build an ideology that focused on shared ideas and on the future. The absence of what many consider essential to national identity—common origin, religion, history—became the impetus for building a brand of civic nationalism that derived from intellectual property rather than the materials of ethnic and historic community. Americans would define their nation not as a "people" whose past justified national sovereignty but as a new set of principles, an experiment in a new form of government. Shared principle and interest became the main criteria for membership in the national community. A nation without a past made the future its justification for being.

INTERNATIONAL NATIONALISM

The "shot heard round the world" was indeed part of a broad transatlantic movement of ideas and people that aimed at creating new nations and also a new social order. Liberal nationalism during the nineteenth century was, above all, international in scope and purpose. Ideas that flowed from Europe to fuel revolution in North America moved back across the Atlantic to ignite another revolution in France and from there to Haiti, Mexico, and down into South America, back to Greece and through Europe. Liberal nationalism transcended political boundaries and went beyond mere goals of national independence and unification to advance ideas of human equality, universal natural rights, and liberation from despotism and slavery. Nationalism, in its youth, was cosmopolitan, liberal, humanitarian, and above all international.[20]

Giuseppe Mazzini, the founder of Young Italy (1831) and leading sprit of Italian unification, was deeply involved in the global humanitarian project that came to be associated with nationalism. He exchanged thousands of letters with his counterparts in the Americas and Europe. He admired the United States as the leading nation "in the onward march of mankind . . . in the great battle which is being fought throughout the world between right and wrong, justice and arbitrary rule, equality and privilege, duty and egotism, republic and monarchy, truth and lies."[21] Among his correspondents were the leading abolitionists of America and England, including Theodore Dwight Weld, to whom he wrote in 1859: "We are fighting the same sacred battle for freedom and the emancipation of the oppressed,—you, Sir, against *negro*, we against *white* slavery. The cause is truly identical." "Do not forget," he admonished an English abolitionist, "whilst at work for the emancipation of the black race, the millions of white slaves, suffering, struggling, expiring in Italy, in Poland, in Hungary, throughout all Europe," which he said was "desecrated by arbitrary, tyrannical power, by czars, emperors, and popes."[22]

Giuseppe Garibaldi, the man of action to Mazzini's man of ideas, spent his lifetime in Italy, South America, the United States, and France either fighting wars of liberation against tyrants, kings, and clergy or in exile from those enemies. It was during one dark interlude in Garibaldi's career that emissaries of President Abraham Lincoln approached him with an invitation to serve in the Union army. Garibaldi accepted on two conditions: that he be given complete command of the Union armed forces and be allowed to declare emancipation of the slaves as the war aim. This offer was

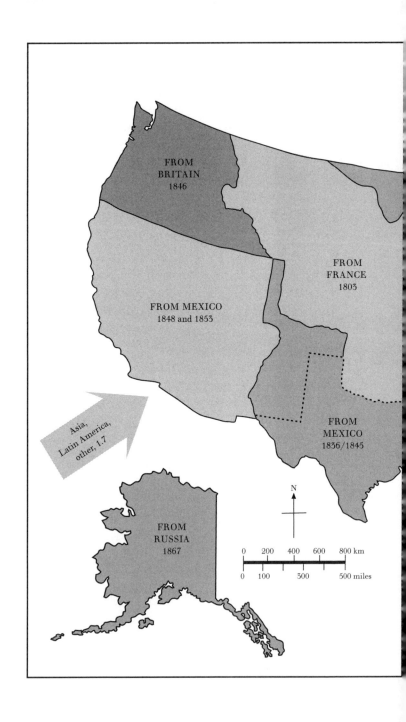

FROM
BRITAIN
1846

FROM
FRANCE
1803

FROM MEXICO
1848 and 1853

Asia,
Latin America,
other, 1.7

FROM
MEXICO
1836/1845

N

FROM
RUSSIA
1867

| 0 | 200 | 400 | 600 | 800 km |
| 0 | 100 | 300 | | 500 miles |

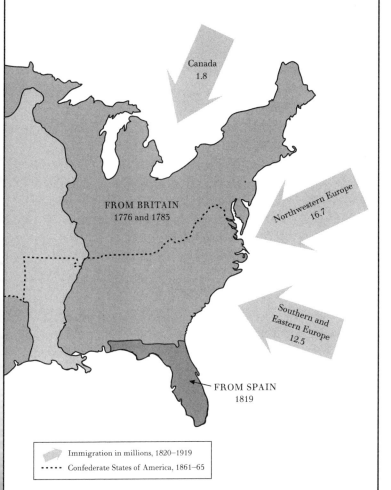

The Making of the
United States of America

Canada
1.8

FROM BRITAIN
1776 and 1783

Northwestern Europe
16.7

Southern and
Eastern Europe
12.5

FROM SPAIN
1819

Immigration in millions, 1820–1919
Confederate States of America, 1861–65

Based on "Expansion of the United States, 1783–1898," copyright Hammond,
Inc., and figures adapted from David Ward, *Cities and Immigrants* (New York:
Oxford University Press, 1971). Numerous land cessions by Native American
nations and the annexation of Hawaii to the United States are not indicated.

The Making of United Italy

Based on "The Unification of Italy" in Christopher Duggan, *A Concise History of Italy* (Cambridge: Cambridge University Press, 1994).

declined, but later in 1863, after the Emancipation Proclamation, Garibaldi wrote to Lincoln:

> In the midst of your titanic struggle, permit me, as another among the free children of Columbus, to send you a word of greeting and admiration for the great work you have begun. . . . You are a true heir of the teaching given us by Christ and by John Brown. If an entire race of human beings, subjugated into slavery by human egoism, has been restored to human dignity, to civilization and human love, this is by your doing and at the price of the most noble lives in America. It is America, the same country which taught liberty to our forefathers, which now opens another solemn epoch of human progress. And while your tremendous courage astonishes the world, we are sadly reminded how this old Europe, which also can boast a great cause of liberty to fight for, has not found the mind or heart to equal you.[23]

Garibaldi was addressing an embattled fighter for liberation, one to another, who happened to be on the other side of the Atlantic. Nationalism for both of them became much more than just independence and unification. Theirs was part of a broad humanitarian campaign that knew no political limits and no boundaries of ethnicity or race.

MAKING ITALY

If Americans worked at defining their new nation by its future *promise*, nationalists in Italy more often sought justification for their national claim by reference to a glorious *past* in ancient Rome and the Renaissance. The Italians called their struggle for national independence and unification the *Risorgimento*, implying that modern Italy was to be a "resurgence" of something that came before, something destined to live again once foreign intruders were cast off. Mazzini spoke of building the "Third Rome" that would succeed the Rome of the Caesars and the Rome of the popes, a capital and a nation devoted to its new mission in the world as a model of liberal humanitarianism. Others looked to Italy's Renaissance for the glory they wanted to resurrect in the new Italy. These versions of an Italian past required a romantic imagination. Ancient Rome, an empire based on conquest and subjugation, was hardly a model for a modern nation. The glory of Renaissance Italy was undeniable, but it flourished during a time of tremendous discord and war among rival city-states. Those hill towns and walled cities that modern tourists find so charming were the product of a terrifying insecurity among a people plagued by marauding armies and brigands in the countryside.[24]

America won independence from British rule, and then, by way of treaties, wars, and expulsion, between the 1780s and 1840s the new nation wrested control of the hinterland from Spain, France, Britain, Native Americans, and Mexicans. The Italians, in contrast, had to dislodge several different "foreign" rulers between 1859 and 1870: Austrians in the North, Spanish Bourbons in the South, and finally the French troops defending Rome and the Papal States in central Italy.

Furthermore, the Italian Risorgimento involved the unification of regions profoundly divided by customs, dialects, and enmities that had developed during a long history of separate city-states, foreign rule, and isolation from one another. Only a small fraction of the population living in the Italian peninsula spoke modern Italian; the rest spoke regional dialects that were often completely incomprehensible to one another.[25]

The nationalism of the Risorgimento was primordial insofar as it harkened back to an ancient, if interrupted, past, but it did not claim to be based on ethnic or cultural homogeneity. Still, the idea of a united Italy acquired a mystical significance that went well beyond simple military or economic advantages. Unification was deemed essential to the idea of a resurgent Italian civilization—if not people—reclaiming some ancient sense of nationhood. Even romantic Italian nationalists such as Mazzini were all too aware of the legacy of hatred and divisiveness among localities. Domination by foreign powers that had invaded from all directions for centuries was as much a product as a cause of Italy's internal fragmentation. As one army officer explained to Stendahl in the early nineteenth century: "Each city detests its neighbours, and is mortally detested in return." This was exactly the reason, he went on to explain, why Italy's foreign invaders had no difficulty dividing and ruling.[26] "Brothers of Italy," implores the national anthem composed in 1847, "we are ready for death, Italy calls." "For centuries we have been downtrodden, and derided, because we are not a people, because we are divided." "Let's gather around one flag, one hope."[27]

Italian nationalists such as Carlo Cattaneo warned that regional differences and uneven development within Italy were so deeply embedded that unification would require an oppressive central state. He urged instead that Italy adopt the Swiss or American model of federalism, granting regions more autonomy while they developed their economies and education so that later they might merge into a unified Italian nation. But Mazzini would have none of this, for federalism, he feared, would only perpetuate the divisiveness of the Italian people and invite further foreign incursions. Unification was essential precisely because without it Italians would fall to quarreling among themselves; one united nation inspired by its historic mission would lift selfish citizens into a community of patriots capable of defending themselves.[28] For Mazzini, the united state would come first, then the nationalism of an imagined Italian community.

Italy was among the last of the major Western European nations to emerge in the age of nationalism. The beginnings of Italy's Risorgimento are usually associated with Napoleon's invasion of the northern peninsula in 1796 and with it the assault on the Old Regime. Between 1796 and 1859 Italian nationalism suffered repeated failures on the practical level, but on the intellectual and cultural levels some degree of nationalism was taking hold, at least among the elites and middle classes. One significant sign of this was the growing popularity of Giuseppe Verdi's operas during the 1840s and 1850s. The popularity of Verdi, a native of Milan, rose during the Austrian occupation of Lombardy. His opera *Nabucco* (1842) dealt with the history of the Hebrews enslaved in Babylon. This and other operas treated historical subjects as thinly veiled protests against foreign oppression of Italy by Austria. According to legend, Italian patriots would rise to their feet and sing along with the chorus of the Hebrew slaves in *Nabucco*. For Italians in Lombardy especially, the chorus became an underground anthem protesting the rule of Austrians. Some sang Verdi's operas in the streets and put his name up on buildings, which became a code for Italian liberation, "Viva VERDI" served as an acronym for "Viva Vittorio Emanuele Re d'Italia."

Whatever its inspiration, Italian nationalism was sufficient to spark numerous popular uprisings against the Bourbons in the South and Austrians in the North but insufficient to guarantee more than fleeting success. A series of abortive revolutions occurred between 1800 and the 1850s, notably in 1848, when Mazzini established the short-lived Republic of Rome. In 1859 the Italian peninsula remained divided into several states ruled either by foreign powers or local sovereigns. The Kingdom of Piedmont, which included Sardinia and Liguria, was ruled by Victor Emmanuel II of the House of Savoy. Lombardy and Venetia were ruled by the Austrians, while the duchies of Parma, Modena, and Tuscany were also controlled indirectly by the Austrians. Rome and the Papal States were defended by French troops. To the south the Spanish branch of the Bourbon family ruled the "Kingdom of the Two Sicilies" (Naples and Sicily). No wonder that Metternich, the ruler of the Austrian Empire, once contemptuously referred to Italy as nothing more than a "geographic expression."

It was clear to all but the most die-hard followers of Mazzini that their plan to bring liberal republicanism to Italy solely through popular revolutions had failed. Italy's claim to nationhood would depend on foreign intervention and its most powerful kingdom, Piedmont. In 1859 France's Napoleon III allied with the Piedmont king, Victor Emmanuel II, in a victorious campaign that ousted the Austrians from Lombardy but not Venice. Lombardy, Parma, Modena, Tuscany, and portions of the Papal States, following popular uprisings against the pope, all elected to unite with Piedmont. In compensation to their French allies, Piedmont ceded its control of Nice and Savoy to France. Making Italy, it seemed, was more a matter of international diplomacy than popular nationalism from below.

It was partly because of his outrage over the cession of his native land, Nice, that Garibaldi took the Risorgimento south in 1860. He led an expedition of volunteer soldiers known as "the Thousand" to liberate Sicily and Naples from Spanish Bourbon rule. Though he did so in the name of Victor Emmanuel and United Italy, it was not with the approval or support of either. Nonetheless, Garibabldi and the Thousand won stunning military victories against a Bourbon army that vastly outnumbered them. By October 1860 they had taken Sicily, then Naples, and the former Bourbon Kingdom of the Two Sicilies became part of United Italy by plebiscite. In March 1861 the United Kingdom of Italy began life, and the first parliament met in Turin, the new nation's capital.

Venetia in the Northeast would become part of Italy in 1866 when Italy allied with Prussia during the Austro-Prussian War. In what Italians call the Third War of Independence the Italian army met disastrous defeat at the hands of the Austrians, but in a complicated diplomatic ploy France received Venetia then ceded it to Italy at the end of the war. Again, French allies were making Italy by diplomacy. The addition of Rome and the Papal States, without which "United" Italy remained cut in two, was not fully accomplished until 1870, when Italian forces blasted through the walls of Rome. Even then the borders of Italy in the Northeast surrounding Trieste and the Tyrol would remain in dispute with Austria until after World War I when the victorious allies forced cession to Italy. After centuries of domination by outside forces, Italy was "made" between 1859 and 1870 for all practical purposes. The geographic expression "Italy" had become a political expression.

To a large extent the making of Italy meant the annexation of provinces into the Kingdom of Piedmont ruled by Victor Emmanuel II and his prime minister Camillo Cavour. It was the Piedmont army, with French and Prussian aid, in the North and Garibaldi's Thousand in the South that did most of the work; the Italian masses were only peripherally involved. Italy's famous political theorist Antonio Gramsci would later explain the weakness of the Italian political system by the limited popular involvement in the original making of Italy. It was a "passive revolution" imposed from above by the Piedmont monarchy and its moderate-conservative followers.[29] As each new territory was wrested from the Austrians, the Bourbons, and the Papal States, the Italian authorities took pains to stage elaborate plebiscites in which citizens elected to join the new nation, but these were largely for show. In Naples citizens were asked to vote not on whether to annex their country to Piedmont and its monarch but instead to approve of "Italia Una Vittorio Emanuele." The plebiscite in Naples took place in full public view in the central piazza, and enormous majorities approved the unification. But this was hardly a popular mandate, for the franchise was restricted to literate, wealthy taxpayers who amounted to a very small fraction of the total population.[30]

One of the most important sources of national identity, as the American example illustrated, was the very struggle for liberation from foreign rule. But in Italy this was more problematic not only because of the multiplicity of foreign powers occupying the peninsula but also because of the ambiguity as to just who was foreign and who was Italian. Language was not a determining signifier of *italianità* ("Italianness"). Piedmont, the region that dominated the making of modern Italy, was largely French-speaking. Both King Victor Emmanuel II and Prime Minister Cavour spoke Italian as a third language, and not very well, according to some observers. The Bourbons, though Spanish in origin, had adapted to local customs and language with great facility since establishing their rule in 1735. Even today one sees the flag of the Bourbons displayed publicly in Naples as a rebuke to their Italian rulers to the north. As for Rome and the Papal States, the French troops were there to protect the church, whose pope and other leaders were for the most part Italian in culture but adamantly opposed to the liberal nationalists.

To be Italian, as the nationalists defined it, meant that one supported the unification of Italy and embraced *italianità* in all its dimensions. "Are you Italians?" asked the Revolutionary Catechism used to drill soldiers in the campaign against the Austrians. "We are by the grace of God," was the prescribed answer. To be Italian, the catechism went on, "means to be born on Italian soil, of an Italian mother, by an Italian father." Beyond that, the signifier of being Italian was "hatred of the German [meaning Austrian] tyrant, hatred which must show in the face, in the bearing, in our words and actions."[31]

Having an alien "them" could define a national "we Italians" or "we Americans." Resentment and hatred of the foreign ruler often served as potent fuel for nationalism in the modern world. In the Americas and in Europe the making of new nations was born in precisely this will to be one against the *other*, the oppressor, the "foreigner." Only then could a people have its own nation and state. Italy, like America, was an idea, and the struggle for independence and unification was only the first step in realizing that idea. Opposition to the "foreign" ruler may have been a necessary prerequisite to nationhood, and the struggle for independence and unification provided its own powerful incentive to nationalism among the leaders and masses of these new nations. Making a new nation was but the first step; making nationals would be an ongoing struggle. America and Italy had been made; now the task would be to make Americans and Italians.

3

The Daily Plebiscite

The making of new nations was not a once-and-for-all event to be finished with the achievement of independence and statehood. National identity and loyalty often took hold slowly, unevenly, and incompletely among the citizenry. Each new generation, each new wave of immigrants, meant that nationbuilding would be an ongoing project. Nations had to cultivate a loyal citizenry that would support the state, pay taxes, obey laws, and fight wars—and not fight each other. Wherever sovereignty rested on the consent of its citizens a modern nation could never take their loyalty for granted. "A nation's existence," wrote the nineteenth-century French scholar Ernest Renan, is a "daily plebiscite."[1]

Much of the new thinking on nationalism has tended to portray national identity as something imposed from above by political or intellectual elites. "Imagined communities" and "invented traditions" had to be fabricated, the argument goes, to persuade an otherwise indifferent or even hostile citizenry of their organic unity as a people, their shared national character, their distinctiveness, or their superiority over other nations. Underlying this view, as I argued in the previous chapter, is disgust with the chauvinism, imperialism, racism, and repression that many lay at the door of nationalism at the end of a bloody century. Also at work is a certain dismay among intellectuals that nationalism continues to inspire

people in a way that few other ideological programs, such as international socialism or feminism, somehow fail to do. If the elites
who invented and fostered nationalism are evil or self-serving in
purpose, by implication the masses who worship this idol are mere
dupes. The main thrust of this revisionist view of nationalism,
in Robert Wiebe's words, comes from a belief in "the moral and
intellectual emptiness of nationalist programs, the imbecility of
their mass followings, and the suffocating effects of nationalism's
success."[2]

Because much of the new scholarship on nationalism assumes
a top-down dissemination of national identity, we rarely see the
people who embrace (or reject) national identity. Consequently, we
have no way of understanding how it is nurtured in citizens and
why nationalism became such a powerful and popular belief. Re-
calling Jerry Gage's patriotic celebration of Columbus and American freedom and his death for the Confederate South, are we to
explain him simply as a young, impassioned man caught up in the
idiocy of nationalism? If so, he had a lot of company, not just in
the Confederate and Union armies but wherever men and women
sacrificed for their country.

Instead of seeing nationalism as an idea or sentiment constructed
by elites and foisted upon the masses, it may be more useful to see
it as something meeting needs that people felt on their own. Few
historical studies have dealt with how citizens come to identify
themselves as nationals, so my generalizations here must remain
tentative. But my limited exploration of this subject in America and
Italy suggests that nationalism in the nineteenth-century variety
did not always originate from the top, that is, through agencies of
the state, the press, or intellectual elites. Instead, it seems that when
the state *tried* to impose some official program to instill nationalist sentiment in the citizenry, it very often failed. Citizens of new
nations did not just adopt a new national identity as they might put
on a uniform. They were either receptive or unreceptive according

to their own interpretation of what the nation meant to them, to their families, and to their way of life.

Those, like Gellner, who understand nationalism as a product of modernization would have us see this juggernaut of change pushing aside traditional values and modes of living in favor of the rational, scientific ways of the modern world. Modernization, like nationalism, is always something that happens *to* people; they may reject or embrace it but never shape it. These "plastic populations," Wiebe notes, "never seem able to resist their leaders' shaping hands."[3] We never see citizens accepting, rejecting, or modifying the new values and identities that transform new nations.

An important exception is Eugen Weber's *Peasants into Frenchmen* (1976), which shows how national integration of such things as transportation, communication, and education materially improved the daily lives of French peasants and altered their consciousness—provincial villagers became Frenchmen. "Roads, railroads, schools, markets, military service, and the circulation of money, goods, and printed matter . . . swept away old commitments, instilled a national view of things in regional minds, and confirmed the power of that view by offering advancement to those who adopted it."[4] Weber's treatment of nation building in France ought to serve as a model for similar studies in other countries, but its ground-level emphasis on the material benefits of national integration go against the reigning view of national identity as something constructed and imposed from above.[5]

By looking at the popular reception of nationalism instead of its elite propagation, we can see that the nationalist project was most successful where it absorbed and complemented popular values instead of battling them for preeminence. Rather than insisting that loyalty to the nation supersede family ties, nationalism invited people to imagine their nation as a vast, extended kinship, a family writ large and one capable of protecting and benefiting domestic life. Mothers of the Republic, fratelli d'Italia, or Sons of Liberty were nationalist appellations that insinuated familial relations among citizens whose duty required devoted love and sacrifice to *la patria*, the fatherland, or mother country. Nationalism, Robert Wiebe writes, coincided with the rise of mass migration that "demanded new concepts of human connectedness." It, in practical effect, "multiplied the people—the kin—on whom one might lay a claim."[6] The nation became an extended family that promised support to its members.

Likewise, nationalism past and present is often seen in conflict with religion. Church and state are pitted against each other in a contest over the fealty of their subjects, particularly in Catholic, Muslim, and other non-Protestant countries. Ernest Gellner puts this graphically when he tells us that Western nationalism sprang from Enlightenment thinkers whose main ambition was "to see the last king throttled with the entrails of the last priest."[7] There was serious conflict between church and state in the Catholic countries of Europe—especially Italy—but nationalism everywhere seemed to advance most successfully when it wrapped itself in religious rhetoric and symbolism and welded national goals to religious mission. Thus the vehemently anticlerical Giuseppe Garibaldi nevertheless became cast as a Christ-like cult figure in Italy, "San Giuseppe," patron saint of the new nation.[8]

America's self-image as God's chosen people transcended its religious origins in the Puritans to become a hallmark of nineteenth-century nationalist thought. The newspaper editor John L. O'Sullivan extended this concept to justify westward expansion and conquest when he wrote in 1845 that America's "manifest destiny" was "the right . . . to possess the whole of the continent which Providence has given us for the development of the great experiment of liberty." Manifest Destiny was the American equivalent to *Italia Unità*, a mission to fulfill God's plan for the nation. Where nationalism, the new civil religion, failed to reconcile with tradi-

tional religious values, it was weaker for it. The Italian state, as we
will see, learned this lesson the hard way.

"We have made Italy," goes one famous expression of nationalist aspiration, "now we must make Italians." This quotation is employed frequently because it neatly captures not only the aware-
ness that a strong national consciousness was *lacking* but also the
necessity and the *will* to do something about it. It also locates the
responsibility for making the nation in the "we," presumably the
leaders of the country. It is worth explaining that this famous quote
attributed to Massimo d'Azeglio was never written or said by him
in quite that way. According to the historians Simonetta Soldani
and Gabriele Turi, the expression became popularized much later
following a disastrous military defeat in 1896 at Adua, during the
Italian campaign in Ethiopia. The humiliation of Adua provoked a
severe crisis among Italian leaders, and Ferdinando Martini, former
minister of public instruction, blamed the debacle there on a failure
of patriotism among Italian soldiers. Martini's version of d'Azeglio's
dictum went: "Fatta l'Italia bisogna fare gli Italiani," which would
translate into English: "Having made Italy requires making Italians." This has been quoted in so many variations in both Italian
and English that it has now taken on an authenticity all its own.

Most interpretations of d'Azeglio's comment are more optimistic
and more imperative than what he actually said. His memoirs,
published posthumously in 1867, include in the preface a lengthy
lament about the failure of Italian character. "The most dangerous enemies of Italy are not the Germans, they are the Italians";
"Why?" d'Azeglio asked. "Because the Italians have willed to make
a new Italy, and they remain the old Italians of before." He finished
by saying bluntly, "Unfortunately Italy is made, but Italians are
not made."[9] In fact, d'Azeglio was decidedly pessimistic about the
prospect of creating an integrated Italian nation, and he went to
his grave regretting the annexation of the South. "Believe me," he

wrote to one confidant, "to make an Italy out of Italians one must not be in a hurry: there will be worse to come, but we shall not see the end."[10]

What d'Azeglio understood, and what those who misquoted him often failed to grasp, is that "we," meaning the predominantly Piedmontese leaders of the state, were not capable of simply recasting people in new national molds. Making Italians was not as simple as annexing new territories and peoples. That would take time and sustained effort, as d'Azeglio warned, and it would take a people who recognized a nation worth identifying with. Nationalism became popular as it answered popular needs and complemented existing values. To understand this requires looking at the nation from the ground level, where nationalism was received, shaped, embraced, or rejected by citizens. Nowhere is the popular reception of nationalism more plainly on view than in public holidays designed to glorify the founding of the new nation.

AMERICA'S NATIONAL SABBATH

Given its short history, its polyglot population, its weak central government, and its vast and expanding boundaries, the United States was challenged more than most nations in forging a national community. If the sprawling, churning jumble of peoples that poured into this expanding national vessel seemed like an unimaginable community, America was nonetheless able to generate remarkable expressions of patriotic fervor and intense national loyalty. At no time was this more evident than on the Fourth of July, when Americans recapitulated the revolution that made them a nation and recited their loyalty to its ideals.

America's Independence Day celebration eventually came to be one of the most significant means of translating the idea of America as a nation, an imagined community of fellow believers, into a palpable, shared experience. The Fourth of July offered several

outstanding virtues. First, it was a day that memorialized the specific event by which the new nation came to be. It was, however,
much more a celebration of *ideas* than it was of heroic *deeds* associated with the Revolution—a "feast of the mind" in the words of
one patriot.[11]

This feast of ideas was highly accessible and in ways that were
almost entirely independent of what Benedict Anderson calls "print
capitalism." America's Independence Day was a performance of
nationalist culture that depended heavily on visual symbols of nationhood and recitations that orally conveyed political ideas and
history to citizens of every rank and age.

Early Independence Day celebrations, according to the historian Len Travers, typically began with a procession of local citizens, all carefully organized, usually led by local civic authorities,
then groups of tradesmen, with citizens falling in toward the end.
In large cities, like Philadelphia, the procession began in 1788 with
a "pageant-play" depicting events from the Revolution through
to the adoption of the Constitution, all with a decidedly pro-
Federalist purpose. Twelve axmen and a troop of cavalry led the
parade and behind them "Independence," a man on horseback carrying a white flag labeled "Fourth of July, 1776," a cap of liberty
atop the staff. Other mounted men represented key events in the
Revolution, one the "French Alliance" carrying a flag with fleurs-
de-lis, another the "Definitive Treaty of Peace" carrying a staff
with olive branches. The thirteenth unit in the parade was "the
Constitution," led by three judges in their robes on "a lofty orna-
mental car" in the shape of an eagle drawn by six white horses.
One judge held a staff that supported a framed copy of the Constitution, topped by a cap of liberty. Banners indicated the dates of
the historic events they symbolized, forming, in Travers's words,
a "moving lesson in history and civics." The grandest unit of the
procession that day was a float representing the new Constitution,
a "New Roof, or Grand Federal Edifice" with thirteen columns

supporting a dome, atop of which was a figure of "plenty, bearing a cornucopia" all drawn by ten white horses. The real crowd pleaser came thirty-second in the procession. It was the "Federal Ship *Union,*" an enormous model ship mounted on a carriage drawn by horses with a canvas skirt covering the wheels and painted to represent water. An admiring crowd, "which up to this time had observed the procession in respectful and awestruck silence," one Philadelphian noted, "gave way to cheers."[12]

This procession was much more elaborate than most, for it was a Federalist celebration of the newly ratified Constitution. But in its use of symbols and pageantry it exemplified the cultural enactment of nationalism in ways that involved the people both as spectators and participants. Usually the procession was followed by an oration and the reading of the Declaration of Independence, then by communal feasting, preceded by an elaborate series of toasts commemorating the ideas and men behind the day. Chief among the events of the day was the oration, which many likened to a sermon. Indeed, the oration often took place inside a church and was accompanied by group prayer. The entire ritualistic style of the celebration lent an air of piety to the new civil religion of the young republic.[13]

The city of Boston left nothing to chance in 1783, when it enacted an ordinance outlining the essential components of a proper Independence Day oration. The oration was required to cover the causes of the Revolution, the "distinguished Characters" who led it, and an honest bow to the "vital aid" of the French. It was intended not simply to provide a history lesson but also to educate its listeners in the "superior advantages" of republican government and the "supreme importance of maintaining personal and public virtue, 'good manners,' and the appropriate education without which all that had been gained would be lost."[14]

By the fiftieth anniversary of independence in 1826 this holiday had taken on a central importance as the "National Sabbath" of the new civil religion. The Fourth of July "became literally the holy day of obligation for American patriots," writes the historian John F. Berens.[15] It was on that day that both Thomas Jefferson and John Adams, two venerable Founding Fathers, died within hours of each other, a coincidence that Americans interpreted as providential and as a symbolic end of partisan division.[16] By this time, the celebration of the Fourth of July had settled into a predictable script followed by small towns in every corner of the nation. It was, above all, a public event organized and performed on the local level, within a community that was very real. Though the typical celebration was far less elaborate than the Philadelphia extravaganza described above, it involved a large array of citizens, male and female, adults and children, whether they took part in the public procession or simply watched. Perhaps most striking about this national holiday is that it did not descend from the national government or even from the state level.[17]

This day of national commemoration would become a contested field within which a variety of divisive issues would play out. The rise of the first and second party systems brought partisan rancor into play. As the quiet solemnity of the nation's "Sabbath" gave way to more raucous expressions of gaiety and disorder, the Fourth of July also became a battleground in the temperance crusade. By the 1840s temperance reformers sought to ban all spirits and introduce cold water toasts. This helped drive a wedge between religious Protestants and German and Irish immigrants.

From the outset, civic leaders worried that the community solidarity they idealized in the young nation was slipping away as partisan, class, ethnic, and then sectional conflict divided Americans even as they celebrated their birth as a nation. But as the historian David Waldstreicher has argued, such conflict did not spell the failure of nationalism as community; it was through these contests over the meaning of the nation that the ideology of nationalism was forged.[18] What is more striking than the dissension itself is that dissenting groups split off to celebrate their own Fourth of July. Irish and German immigrants, who resented temperance regulations or the Protestant religious tone of the celebration would organize celebrations that they controlled. Likewise, in the South following the Civil War the Fourth of July became a day for joyous celebration of freedom among blacks and one shunned by most whites.[19]

Americans made Independence Day a national holiday experienced locally. North and South, East and West, they followed a similar script and ritual. Whatever relative importance some placed on prayer and oration versus beer and barbecue, each Fourth of July embraced a broad social spectrum cf Americans. Though local celebrations reflected the ethnic and racial fissures in the community, those celebrating the Fourth envisioned a kinship to one another and to hundreds of other communities across the country celebrating in similar ways, and they imagined links across time to the events and people of 1776.[20] For the American nation that is when the past began.

THE STATUTO FIASCO

In several important ways the process of nation building in Italy might seem less formidable than it was in the United States. In contrast to America, Italy had a *past*, a well-defined geographical *place*, and a long-settled *people*. Indeed, the Risorgimento made the past the central theme of Italy's claim to nationhood. The boundaries of the new Italian nation by 1870 were comparatively stable and clearly defined by high mountains setting off a bootlike peninsula and two major islands from the European continent. Few incoming foreign migrants crossed those borders, though a large flow out of Italy, especially the South, began after unification.

The problem lay with the diversity of peoples within those well-defined borders and their weak attachment to the new nation and to *italianità*. The challenge of "making Italians," which meant literally creating a common language, culture, and identity among the disparate peoples from North to South, was daunting. The northern leaders of the newly united Italy were keenly aware of the lack of strong national identity and the urgent need to establish a popular base for the legitimacy of the new state.

The Italian state was far more assertive than the American government in its myriad attempts to stimulate national identity. Though the myth of the Risorgimento held that the new nation reawakened a dormant *italianità*, political leaders were painfully aware of the great diversity of language, customs, and identities that persisted in Italy. Linguistic fragmentation involved much more than different pronunciation or idiomatic expressions, as was true of American regional accents, for the dialects of Italy employed different vocabularies as well. Such commonplace references as the days of the week had entirely different words from one region to the next. Only about 2.5 percent of the population in 1860 was thought to speak and understand Italian, that is, the dialect of Tuscany that became the standard for educated Italians.[21] Nationalists in Italy were painfully aware that language was but a superficial sign of profound diversity and division among its people.

With mixed success, the new state attempted to enlist citizens in the new civil religion of nationalism through public holidays and commemorations. Perhaps the most revealing example was the ill-fated Statuto or Constitution Day, promulgated as a national holiday in 1861 to celebrate the statute of 1848. Though the constitution remained the supreme law of the United Kingdom of Italy for a century (until Italy elected to become a republic in 1947), this holiday asked citizens to celebrate an event that antedated the founding of modern Italy and underlined the Piedmont hegemony. It was not a great concession to popular democracy in any case;

King Charles Albert, father of Victor Emmanuel II, had granted the statute in March 1848 with great reluctance and only in the face of revolutionary upheaval.

Alternative holidays commemorating the modern nation's founding might have celebrated the famous victories of Garibaldi and the Thousand in the South. But conservative monarchists wanted to do nothing to encourage democratic revolutionary claims on the soul of Italy by honoring Garibaldi, much less the South. They chose instead to locate the origins of the new Italy in the monarchy, the House of Savoy, in Piedmont, and in the rule of law. Marco Minghetti, minister of the interior, explained that one could not find in Italian history a unique event that marked the unification of Italy, comparable to France's Bastille Day. It made sense therefore to conserve the festival of the Statuto that had been celebrated in Turin since 1851. Among the first pieces of business enacted by the new Parliament that met in Turin in 1861 was the creation of Statuto Day as a national holiday. "The force of this communion of thought, of affection and of purpose," explained Minghetti, ". . . that binds a people, that which in a single day . . . returns to God the gratitude of having obtained that which for so many centuries was vainly desired; and that communion reinforces the consciousness of real greatness."[22]

The capriciousness of this invented tradition was accentuated by the decision to name the first Sunday in June as the new national holiday. The Statuto had been granted March 4, 1848, but there was concern that the rainy weather that time of year—in Piedmont at least—might dampen patriotic ardor. The choice of Sunday as a national holiday was intended to merge secular and religious sentiments, but it met with hostility from the church, which continued to oppose the new state of Italy. Pope Pius IX denounced the entire liberal national enterprise and, in effect, excommunicated the government of the Italian state. He warned Catholics not to vote in state elections or to support the state voluntarily in any way.

Now the church called on its followers to turn their backs on the festival of the secular state and come to church on Sunday.[23]

Besides opposition from the church, the Statuto failed as a popular holiday for the simple reason that citizens were not involved except as spectators of the new state's pompous military parades. Instead of a celebration that invited participation from the inhabitants of local communities, the Italian Statuto Day was an occasion on which the majesty of the state presented itself to the public. The typical Statuto festival was staged only in major cities like Turin, Milan, Rome, Naples, and Palermo. It involved lengthy parades of military regiments and government officials watched by a selected audience from the local populace. One letter to the mayor of Turin in 1870 complained that the streets to the parade route were actually closed off and all but government officials were excluded.[24] State officials tried to co-opt the church by arranging for mass to parading soldiers and the singing of the *Te Deum*, the Latin hymn. The procession that followed was accompanied by the national anthem, which was at that time the *Marcia Reale* (Royal March).

The holiday fell into disfavor, both with the public and with the more liberal government that took power in 1876. By the late 1880s the Statuto Day was all but dead as a national holiday. A Catholic journal took pleasure in noting the failure of this secular rival to church authority: "The festival of the Statuto was not a creation but an imitation, that was superimposed on the Christian holiday dedicated to God . . . but the Christian holiday stays, the holiday of the Statuto is spent."[25] The word "fiasco" is of Italian origin, and it is used to refer to an empty wine flask at a feast. The state-sponsored Statuto Day was a fiasco, a flask devoid of meaning for the people who were supposed to imbibe patriotism.

The Italian search for a viable national holiday did not end with the collapse of Statuto Day. Prime Minister Francesco Crispi was greatly concerned about the lack of popular patriotism in Italy. A hero of the Risorgimento and a Sicilian, Crispi led a vigorous program of nation building that encompassed aggressive foreign adventures in Africa and numerous efforts to instill popular patriotism at home. In 1895 he introduced a new national holiday. Known simply as September 20, it paid honor to the day Italian troops breached Porta Pia and took Rome from the pope in the name of Italian unity. Here was another national holiday certain to aggravate the church's opposition to the state, and it too fell into disfavor, particularly after Benito Mussolini's regime reconciled with the church.

It was after the fall of Mussolini that Liberation Day, April 25, was designated a national holiday celebrating the end of Nazi control of Italy. Heralded as the "Second Risorgimento," the Resistance movement echoed the regional bias of the first Risorgimento, which privileged the North as the source of *italianità*. Liberation Day celebrated a resistance movement that had been led by the northern Left. Since Allied forces had invaded Italy from the south and pushed Nazi forces north of Rome, there was no southern participation in the Resistance and therefore little identity with the holiday, which became the property of Communists and Socialists in the North instead of something to share as Italians.

It was with great interest that I attended a community feast (*sagra*) celebrating Liberation Day during the time I was studying this subject in April 2000. I went with friends, including a Sicilian who had never seen a Liberation Day celebration in her hometown of Siracusa. We went to a small town in Tuscany, a strong Communist region of Italy that was not far from the Germans' Gothic Line during the war. There were few survivors of the struggle that took place some sixty years earlier, but the parents and grandparents of these people had taken a prominent role in the Resistance. I went to witness the current Italian equivalent of our Fourth of July, a feast of Italian patriotism, *tortelli* pasta, and *bistecca fiorentina*. We drove deep into the Tuscan countryside, into the Mugello Valley, far from any contamination of tourism or urban sophistication. But upon arriving at the sagra, I was dismayed to find absolutely no sign of the patriotic purpose of the occasion: no flags, no banners, no music, no decorated veterans, no speeches or toasts—nothing to commemorate the historical event this was intended to celebrate. My neighbors later told me that Liberation Day had become nothing more than a *festa di mangiare*, a festival of eating. Finally, it occurred to me that Italians had located the true source of their national pride: food and the pleasures of sharing it together as a community. An Italian patriotism of pasta may constitute a civil religion few nations can rival.

SCHOOLING AMERICANS

Perhaps the most visible hand of the state in molding its citizens can be seen at work in the public schools, where young and impressionable citizens could be taught the unique virtues of being nationals. How well I remember from my own youth in the Cold War era beginning each school day by standing, facing the American flag, placing our hands over our hearts, and reciting in unison the Pledge of Allegiance. I still recall the day in 1954 during the height of the McCarthy era when we were told that we were now "one nation, *under God*, indivisible" (a revision advocated by the Knights of Columbus, an Italian American Catholic organization). Rarely did a week go by in grade school that we did not sing the "Star Spangled Banner," "America," and other patriotic songs. We read Edward Everett Hale's account of Phillip Nolan, "The Man without a Country," and stories about George Washington cutting down the cherry tree, stories I believed to be true until an embarrassingly advanced stage of my life. During high school we were treated to courses in "civics," which taught us the evils of communist dictatorships that brainwashed students into thinking theirs was the one best form of society and government. During the Vietnam War we saw how unevenly this nationalist propaganda took hold among members of my generation, but it was not for want of effort by our schools.

In the early American republic educators were no less concerned about instilling national identity and loyalty in the children of the new nation. In the public schools and the textbooks they assigned we can see the most deliberate efforts to shape the minds of young Americans. New England took the lead, just as New England and the Northeast generally became the leading force in shaping American national identity at nearly every front.[26] The historian Susan-Mary Grant makes a persuasive case for "Northern nationalism" emerging by the 1830s to claim a salient role as the source of American ideals and traits.[27] The leading role of the northeastern urban population in developing public education and publishing school textbooks and popular magazines reinforced this formative role in shaping American national identity. Because of its limited public schooling and widespread illiteracy, the South remained the region least engaged in this intellectual enterprise of nation building. If Benedict Anderson is right about nationalism as an abstraction that is conveyed through print, the American South imbibed less and took a lesser role in defining American nationalism than did the North. But let us return to that thought later.

American educators in the young republic urged an education that was "truly American," writes the historian Lawrence Cremin, one "purged of all vestiges of older monarchical forms" and "rooted in the American soil, based on an American language and literature, steeped in American art, history, and law, and committed to the promise of an American culture." Noah Webster, an ardent cultural nationalist, deplored the poor quality of public instruction in America: "Every child in America should be acquainted with his own country. He should read books that furnish him with ideas that will be useful to him in life and practice. . . . A selection of essays, respecting the settlement and geography of America; the history of the late revolution and of the most remarkable characters and events that distinguished it, and a compendium of the principles of the federal and provincial governments, should be the principal school book in the United States."[28] Webster had already authored just such a book, *An American Selection of Lessons in Reading and Speaking*, first published in 1787. Its subtitle—*Calculated to Improve the Minds and Refine the Taste of Youth. And also to Instruct Them in the Geography, History, and Politics of the United States*—revealed his larger purpose in molding an American moral character. In monarchies, he wrote, limited education geared to social rank made perfect sense, but in a republic where the people were sovereign, education of the poorest citizen was essential. American education ought to aim at character rather than knowledge, Webster argued: "The virtues of men are of more consequence to society than their *abilities*; and for this reason, the *heart* should be cultivated with more assiduity than the *head*."[29]

Webster's readers, spellers, grammars, and other schoolbooks became best-selling texts in the young republic. But his most famous and lasting contribution to American identity involved the language itself. His famous dictionary, *An American Dictionary of the English Language*, first published in 1828, was completely revised according to American principles of practical usage and spelling. We owe it to Webster that "color" and "labor" are spelled as Americans pronounced them. Thanks to Webster, they would begin to form their own standards for what he pointedly called an "American English."

Samuel F. B. Morse, painter, inventor, and nationalist nonpareil, also wrote highly popular school texts on American history that aimed at defining and reassuring American identity. Mason Locke Weems wrote laudatory biographies of Benjamin Franklin, Francis Marion, and George Washington. His famous story of young

Washington chopping down the cherry tree, then confessing to
his father that he "could not tell a lie," became so embedded in
the Washington mythology it hardly mattered that it was nothing more than sheer fabrication by Weems. Another widely popular set of texts, William Holmes McGuffey's *Eclectic Readers*,
combined similar anecdotal accounts of American heroes and constructed stalwart images of American virtue and Old World corruption. "Schoolmaster to the nation," McGuffey saw his readers
become the "portable school for the new priests of the republic."[30]
Young readers of McGuffey, Weems, Morse, and Webster would
be prepared by adulthood to imbibe the nationalist histories of
George Bancroft and the celebratory writings of Ralph Waldo
Emerson.[31]

All these school texts and histories delineated America's special
characteristics, which one author summarized as "generally indus-
trious, intelligent, and enterprising" with an "ardent love of liberty,
courage, and strict morality."[32] In one textbook a pair of engravings illustrated some essential differences between Old and New
World society. In it America is depicted with sturdy workers in the
foreground, prosperous buildings including a domed capitol, com-
mercial ships, and an abundant harvest of grain alongside tools and
books. Europe, in contrast, is captured in a triptych, one showing a
natural disaster, an earthquake; another an aristocratic court scene;
and the third the ruins of what appears to be Roman civilization.[33]
The opposite of America, Europe was old, undemocratic, burdened
by its past, and unblessed by nature.

Because American schooling never became a function of the
national government, its role in making Americans was patchy.
While states in the Northeast and Midwest developed statewide
graded public schools with compulsory attendance laws, in the
South schooling remained a largely private matter until after the
Civil War when centralized state education systems were introduced as part of Reconstruction. Even then the quality and effec-

tiveness of public education varied greatly from state to state, from rural to urban populations, and from one class or ethnic group to another.

Beginning in the mid–nineteenth century, Irish and other Catholic immigrants saw the public schools as a secular or Protestant threat to their religious culture. Several days of rioting erupted in Philadelphia in 1844 when Catholic parents objected to their children being treated to Protestant religious lessons. When they could not control the school boards and install nuns and priests as teachers, Catholics withdrew to their own parochial schools.[34] American public schools would face a far greater challenge in the late nineteenth century when millions of immigrants poured into the nation's large cities. It was out of alarm toward these "new immigrants" that a more muscular program of Americanization was introduced in public schools. The larger purpose of Americanization, in courses designed to teach language, history, and civics, was to instill loyalty to America and dilute identity with the "old country" their parents had left. It was during the 1890s, by no coincidence, that the Pledge of Allegiance was introduced into the schools as a daily ritual of fealty to the nation.

CIVIL CHURCHES

The Italian school, by contrast to the decentralized American model, was the product of the national government and might have become a powerful instrument for nationalizing young Italians and creating a common language and Italian identity. The school, in the words of one Italian leader, was to be a sort of "civil church," for it aimed not only at preempting the traditional monopoly of the church on education but also at instructing the new civil religion of nationalism and secular values.[35] The public school came to be seen as "the only suitable means of planting the sentiment of *italianità* by force in the hearts in which it is absent." Francesco

De Sanctis, the first minister of education, saw it as nothing less than the instrument for transforming "different peoples who do not understand each other" into "a single people."[36]

Italians then and now had remarkable faith in the power of the state to reform society, a faith that was no less fervent for its long history of disappointment. Liberals in Piedmont nationalized public education in 1859 with the Casati Law, which set the course for Italian public education over the next half-century. The law required all communes to provide at least two years of primary schooling for local boys and girls, four years in towns with more than four thousand people. By law all instruction was to be given in the Italian language so students would learn the official language of the state in favor of the regional dialect their families used. Attendance did not become compulsory until the 1877 Coppino Law, which also abolished mandatory religious instruction. This was a major initiative of the new leftist government to use public education to cultivate Italian national identity. In 1882 suffrage reform made literacy the major qualification for males so schooling became directly linked to citizenship. But even then, only two, later three, years of school attendance were required.[37]

The ideal, if not the reality, of the Italian public school was dramatically portrayed in Edmondo De Amicis's popular book *Cuore: Libro per i Raggazzi* (Heart: Book for children), first published in 1886. De Amicis's fictional account of Italian school life became standard fare for Italian schoolchildren and remains so to this day. Set in a primary school in Turin, the northern capital of Piedmont, the book detailed the daily life of an impressionable schoolboy who takes to heart every lesson in the catechism of Italy's new civil religion. Students write essays with such titles as "Why Do I Love Italy?" and many of the monthly lessons focus on heroes of the Risorgimento, with particular emphasis on battlefield courage and sacrifice. Virtue, intelligence, and patriotism are all linked. The school bully is expelled, not for smoking, swearing, or abusing other students but for having laughed at the commemoration of King Victor Emmanuel II.

One of the principal themes in De Amicis's book was the importance of mutual respect and tolerance toward all Italians, not least those from the South. In one chapter a boy from the southern province of Calabria joins the class, and the teacher graciously welcomes him as one who "was born in a glorious land which gave Italy illustrious men, and which gives her strong workers and brave soldiers. . . . Cherish him so that he does not think about how far he is from the town in which he was born. Make him see that an Italian boy, no matter which Italian school he sets foot in, finds brothers there." A boy named Derossi, identified as the smartest boy in the class embraces the Calabrian, and he returns the welcome by kissing Derossi on both cheeks. Derossi then turns to the class and says: "our country struggled for fifty years, and thirty thousand Italians died. You must all respect and love one another. If any of you should harm our companion because he was not born in our province, you would make yourself for ever more unworthy of raising your eyes from the ground when the tricolour goes by."[38]

The reality of the Italian public school fell far short of the ideal. Whatever the law said, Italy's public schools were poorly funded and left largely to the control of local municipal authorities. Few schoolteachers in the countryside, especially in the South, could actually speak Italian, so the school often reinforced rather than erased regional dialects. Many peasant families preferred that their children work in the fields, and they resented paying taxes for what they saw as an unnecessary luxury. Truancy went uncontrolled and about 80 percent of the rural southern peasant children avoided schools altogether.[39] In the distance between law and behavior, ideal and practice, the school illustrated the disparity between the legal Italy promoted by the new state and the real Italy its citizens inhabited.

The first national census in 1871 showed that nearly 70 percent of the population could not read or write, and many deemed literate could do little more than write their names. Literacy rates varied by region, class, and sex, of course. Among southern peasants illiteracy was universal, and even in provincial capitals about half the population was illiterate. (Illiteracy in the United States in 1870 was about 10 percent, with much higher rates in the South, especially among former slaves.)[40]

Moreover, there was a long tradition of opposition to public education in Italy from both the church and crown.[41] The Catholic clergy opposed the state's attempt to usurp their role in education; they remained steadfast enemies of the secular schools, encouraging truancy and opposing new compulsory attendance laws. Local schools often compromised with the church by including religious instruction or hiring priests as teachers. To appease the church the state officials instructed schoolteachers to teach their students the "duties that bound them to 'God, to their parents, their brothers and sisters and their country.'"[42] In 1886 the minister of education summarized the limited goals of Italian public education: "We must not forget that the primary school aims at rearing a population as [well] instructed as possible, but principally honest, hardworking, useful to the family and devoted to the Country and to the King."[43]

Despite its deficiencies, education in Italy made progress against illiteracy. By 1911, at the fiftieth anniversary of unification, Italy's illiteracy rate had declined to under 40 percent, though in the southern provinces 60–70 percent remained illiterate.[44] Whatever its limitations among the peasantry, particularly in the South, Italy's public schools had educated and "nationalized" much of the urban, middle-class population, and the university system had done the same for the country's elites.[45] "The school in every commune is a monument of civility," one proud Italian educator wrote in 1865, "in which minds improve altogether more than in the barracks. . . . Aired, cleaned, offering an example of neatness, of order."[46]

FRATERNITY OF WAR

The military offered another state-controlled instrument for nationalizing a crucial element of Italian society. During the 1870s an active conscription policy introduced about one in four Italian males, age twenty, into a national army. Draft dodging, at least in the early years of conscription, was widespread, especially in the South. Wealthy men were allowed to pay for a substitute, which often aggravated class resentment. In the North especially, however, compliance with the draft and voluntary long-term service gave indication that the national idea was taking hold. Military service came to be seen as a badge of honor among many Italian officers and soldiers.[47]

The Italian army was also an important device for imposing state authority on rebellious elements; indeed, it more often served to keep civil order *within* Italy than to defend its borders. For that reason the Italian army had to be especially well disciplined and firmly in the control of conservative, predominantly Piedmontese officers. The army adopted a strict policy of mixing regiments with conscripts from two different provinces who were stationed in a third province. To limit fraternization and sympathy with local citizens, each regiment was stationed in a province for no more than four years before being relocated. "Military barracks and police stations loomed large in the social geography of Italy's towns and cities," writes one historian, "and in rural communities, the headquarters of the *carabinieri* [military police] was frequently the most conspicuous building."[48] During the tumultuous years of the new nation there were dozens of riots, illegal assemblies, strikes, and a serious problem of outlaw brigand bands in the South that prompted the armed intervention of the state. The Italian army was making Italians in more ways than one. Through conscription it pulled thousands of young men out of their villages, exposed them to different regions of the country, and instilled in them national

ideals and patriotism. The military also became the principal instrument for enforcing the authority of the state over its sometimes
unwilling and rebellious citizens.[49]

The military played only a limited and episodic role in
nationalizing Americans before the Civil War. In the young
republic military service during peacetime was confined to a small
corps of professional officers and enlisted men in a poorly equipped
and trained regular army, supplemented by even more inadequate
state militia forces. Going into the War of 1812 the regular army
stood at around eleven thousand men. By the time of the Mexican
War in 1845 this force had declined to a little over seven thousand.
In wartime the United States military had to depend on volunteer
enlistees from the states.[50] The army swelled to over twenty
thousand because of an enormous turnout of volunteers. Both the
War of 1812 and the Mexican War were joined to militaristic
nationalism and territorial expansion in the West. These wars
produced thousands of veterans and officers who by virtue of their
participation in national military ventures had forged an identity
with the larger nation. Furthermore, the repeated success of wars
against the British, Mexicans, and Indians provided a powerful
impetus to American nationalism. Each war produced its celebrated
heroes and victories along with a corps of veterans who gave body
to the national idea. The strength of that national identity for many
southern veterans would be severely tested in 1861.

HEROES AND MONUMENTS

Wars and military victories helped create a pantheon of new national heroes and a narrative of the nation's triumphs. No less
important were monuments to fallen soldiers and tragic defeats.
"Suffering in common unifies more than joy does," Ernest Renan
wrote: "Where national memories are concerned, griefs are of more
value than triumphs, for they impose duties, and require a common

effort."[51] Out of these military struggles, whether triumphal or tragic, new nations could construct a history and tell their story, not to foreigners but to their own citizens.

In schoolbooks and biographies national heroes and national history aimed at reproducing the patriotism of the past. These historical treatments of a nation's history and heroes provide a classic example of the ways a nation could come to be imagined through the medium of print. But the civil religion of nationalism also involved a panoply of shrines that citizens encountered in everyday life. These were nonliterary signifiers of national consciousness in monuments, buildings, and the names of streets, piazzas, and public places. These symbols of the nation and its heroes, like the parades and orations of national holidays, were readily accessible to a broad population regardless of age or education.

In the United States the naming of new places and geographic features offered an ideal opportunity to honor national heroes and create a sense of national identity. As the United States expanded westward the act of naming thousands of new counties, towns, mountains, and rivers offered an unusual opportunity to stamp the national ideal on the very face of the country. Wilbur Zelinsky's careful study "Nationalistic Names on the Land" catalogs the place names of counties and towns. He shows that Washington, Jackson, Lincoln, Jefferson, Franklin, Grant, Madison, Harrison, and Monroe are the leading names of national heroes, while other place names, such as Union, Liberty, Independence, Freedom, and Mount Vernon, conveyed patriotic and inspirational meaning. When these names are plotted on the map, Zelinsky shows, they form a strong nationalistic band of naming stretching across the Northeast to the Midwest and with notably weaker traces in the South and Far West.[52]

Americans were less zealous than Europeans in the building of monuments, statues, and other structures erected to glorify national heroes and national events. Some thought of this idolatry of great men on horseback as an Old World custom unfitting to a republic. For a long time, Zelinsky tells us, "the only durable landscape feature denoting nationalism was the Liberty Tree or, in its literally stripped-down version, the Liberty Pole." One European visitor noted: "In America ... do not look ... for monuments raised to the memory of illustrious men. I know that this people has its heroes: but no where have I seen their statues." He did note that George Washington was the exception that proved the rule, for to him "alone are there busts, inscriptions, column [sic]; this is because Washington in America, *is not a man but a God*."[53] But even a national god had a tough go of it getting a monument raised to him in America. The movement launched to build the Washington Monument raised money dollar by dollar in local communities across the land. The obelisk on the Washington Mall that was begun in 1848 would not be completed until 1885; meanwhile, it stood partially finished as a reminder of how indifferent Americans were to this kind of monumental tribute, even in honor of its most revered hero.[54]

In the daily plebiscite of nationalism, monuments, statues, and memorials could be very powerful visual reminders that citizens belonged to a nation, to something great and enduring. In a country like Italy these symbols of the nation became ubiquitous by the late nineteenth century. Especially after 1876 (when the Left took over the national government) the earlier reliance on state-sponsored holidays gave way to more popular expressions of nationalism.[55] The heroes of the Risorgimento received the most attention. Few new nations could rival the Italians in their zeal for romanticizing their history and honoring its heroes with monuments or place names. One Catholic periodical ridiculed the cult of the state that inundated everyday life: "You pass from one city to another, and in every one always, irrevocably, you are constricted to crossing a XX September that goes to a piazza Plebiscito where you turn into a corso Vittorio Emanuele that opens in a piazza dell'Indipendenza from which one turns into a via Garibaldi from which it turns into a via Cavour."[56] Every Italian city or village offers this daily lesson in national history.

Many less famous figures in the Risorgimento won recognition in street names and public monuments, but the major figures in this symbolic nationalism were King Victor Emmanuel II and Garibaldi. The adulation of each echoed the original division between monarchists and liberal democrats who continued to contest the historical meaning of the Risorgimento.

Garibaldi's battles in the cause of liberty in South America in the 1830s had made him an international "hero of two worlds" long before his triumphant conquest of Sicily and Naples in 1860. Lionized in England, Europe, the United States, and South America, in Italy Garibaldi had been a thorn in the side of the moderate monarchist government. He was a popular proponent of revolutionary nationalism and a rogue guerrilla leader whose military genius (or luck) embarrassed Cavour and other leaders of the state. In 1862 when Garibaldi rallied his men to renew the attack on Rome and complete the unification of Italy, the conservative prime minister Urbano Rattazzi sent the Italian army to stop him. At Aspromonte Garibaldi faced them down standing in front of his men shouting orders not to fire and yelling, "Viva Italia!" The Italian troops were ordered to fire on him, and he fell wounded in the foot and leg. Garibaldi, the liberator of Sicily and Naples, recuperated in an Italian jail.

Garibaldi was also denounced by the Church of Rome as an enemy of the pope and of religion, but his popularity took on a religious significance. He was often depicted in magazines and calendars as a Christ-like figure with his long hair and poncho and his saintly gaze. One cartoon showed San Giuseppe being crucified by the king and his ministers. Bandages from his wounded foot and locks of his hair were treated as religious relics. The foot never healed properly and was popularly interpreted as a stigmata. The

Garibaldi cult became one of the many ways in which the secular, civil religion of nationalism appropriated forms and meanings from traditional religion. Ironically, it was as a figure of opposition to church and king that Garibaldi became such an immensely popular national hero. After the Left took power in 1876, there was more official celebration of Garibaldi by the state, but his power came from the popular cult that had grown up in opposition to state-sponsored nationalism. Rare is the city or even small town in Italy where one does not find some tribute to Garibaldi, if not an equestrian statue at least a street or piazza named in his honor.[57]

Conservative monarchists instead exalted King Victor Emmanuel II as the hero of Italy's Risorgimento and the personification of national ideals. They had less to work with than Garibaldi's devotees in terms of personal character and deeds. Victor Emmanuel II was widely regarded among European state leaders as an "imbecile," and the more he spoke of his political wisdom the more obvious his ignorance became; "he was incapable of writing a single page of literate prose," the historian Denis Mack Smith irreverently informs us. The House of Savoy was the oldest royal dynasty in Europe, and for generations marriage choices had been dictated by diplomacy; and dynastic considerations, according to Mack Smith, "took precedence over eugenics." The king prided himself on being a courageous military leader, and his willingness to engage in heroic assaults was matched by his utter lack of tactical savvy. The king was short and fat with an astonishing mustache that extended a full ten inches across his round face, and his most redeeming quality was his lack of energy and interest for anything but hunting, for he might have been a brutal tyrant otherwise.[58] But monarchs are important for what they symbolize, not what they are, and the monarchists did all they could to make the king a symbol of the new Italy.

Nowhere was the will to build national identity around the king more grandly displayed than in the monument built in the center of Rome, the Vittoriano, the Altar of the Fatherland, more popularly known as the "wedding cake" or "typewriter." It is a gigantic, blinding white marble spectacle that covers the northern side of the Roman Capitoline, rivaling—some would say overwhelming—that ancient center of Roman government. When the king died in 1878 there was an elaborate funeral procession through Rome to the Pantheon where he was interred in that architectural survivor of ancient Rome. Plans began immediately for a modern monument to the king, and it took six years and two international competitions to find the architect, Giuseppe Sacconi. Before it was finished in 1911, on the fiftieth anniversary of the new nation, twenty-six years had passed in building the monument, the costs rising and the design becoming ever more elaborate as it grew.[59] It stands in Rome today, the streets below buzzing with Vespas and Fiats, the monument itself until recently closed off to people except for the soldiers guarding the tomb of the Unknown Soldier, which lies below the king's equestrian statue. In this way the Vittoriano represents perfectly the effort by the state to impose the national ideal from on high, while the people go about their daily plebescite below.

The Vittoriano monument may be an extreme example of the extravagant lengths nationalists were willing to go to in their attempt to impress the national idea upon their citizenry. But it was imitated in different ways in many other nations. America, a country not usually given to monumental excess, did exercise extravagance with its capital city, Washington. The new capital was designed by Pierre-Charles L'Enfant, a French architect who borrowed heavily from Versailles, the royal palace of the late monarchs whose heads had rolled at the guillotine a few years earlier. L'Enfant's 1791 plan proposed to lay out the new American capital "on such a scale as to leave room for that aggrandizement and embellishment which the increase of the wealth of the Nation will permit it to pursue at any period how ever remote."[60] In time, it would fill with imposing buildings, colossal monuments to heroic leaders and events, and statuary celebrating the Manifest Destiny of the young nation. But like the Vittoriano in Rome, this ponderous form of state-sponsored nationalism existed apart from the citizenry who were embracing, or rejecting, their identity as members of a national community according to their own sense of belonging to something they valued on their own terms.

4

Imagined Enemies

The national idea did not always triumph over competing loyalties in the daily plebiscite. Nation building often failed to win the allegiance of opposing ethnic or provincial enclaves. Even after establishing its authority over diverse groups of its citizens, the modern nation often faced opposition from within. Regional antagonism threatened the unity of many nations, few more dramatically than America and Italy.

Italians have always fretted about the weakness of national identity and unity among their people, but United Italy was never seriously challenged by any regional separatist rebellion unless one counts the Northern League. Americans faced continual challenges to national unity and identity. Rapid expansion, vast spaces, and massive immigration of diverse linguistic, religious, and racial groups all made nation building problematic. But full-fledged separatism has only rarely been seized as a remedy in America's contentious mix of peoples.

Social and political conflict is endemic to modern nations, but they became more threatening to national unity when they coalesced in coherent territorial form. Only when a subnational population could see itself first as a region, then as an aggrieved minority, and then as a separate nation—only then did secession become a viable option.

THE OTHER AMERICA

The nationalist ideal of unification and inclusiveness finds its most formidable enemy in its close relative, separatism, for it challenges at a fundamental level a nation's claim to legitimate rule over one people. Paradoxically, nationalism also frequently finds a powerful impetus in the presence—real or imagined—of opposition from within. Nowhere was this more evident than in the peculiar relationship of the South to the nation in America and Italy. Though vastly different in many respects, each South at the inception of national independence was deliberately included in a nation that celebrated its unity as the apotheosis of its destiny. In time, however, each of these southern regions became demonized for being backward, out of phase with the progressive aspirations of the larger nation, and a threat to national well-being.

Though each nation came to judge its South as somehow not belonging, the national commitment to unification remained strong. The Italian state imposed its rule by force in a long and bloody war against outlaw forces that were concentrated in the southern provinces. The Brigands War coincided with the American Civil War in which the Confederacy's bid for nationhood was defeated after a bloody conflict. In each setting the Southern Question eventually found its remedy in various efforts to reconstruct the South. Whether aimed at abolishing slavery or the Mafia or improving the economy, health, and education of the region, all of these reform efforts emanated from a common premise: the South was somehow unlike the rest of the nation and the remedy was to make it less so. The process of vilifying a deviant people or region within a nation and imposing remedies on it provided a powerful source of national identity outside that targeted group or region. The other America, the South, helped define the ideal America, and a bloody war to defend its unity challenged and galvanized the loyalty of citizens, at least those outside the rebellious region.

The southern colonies joined the United States as equal and valued partners in common cause for independence against Britain in 1776. The flourishing export economy of Chesapeake tobacco and South Carolina rice made the South a prosperous and powerful partner. The expansion of the cotton economy in the early nineteenth-century South only strengthened its position as a rich and important region, all the more so as the Northeast came to depend on southern cotton for textile manufactures. One measure of the South's importance was its political power. The Virginia Dynasty that began with President Washington continued through Jefferson, James Madison, and James Monroe. More southern presidents followed—Andrew Jackson, John Tyler, James K. Polk, and Zachary Taylor. During the fifty years after 1800, in no less than forty-two a southern president resided in the White House.[1] The relocation of the nation's capital from Philadelphia and New York to the new city of Washington on the Potomac in 1800 was another bow to southern power. The Constitution was carefully constructed to win southern support, not least with its clause that allowed representation based on three-fifths of the slave population and another protecting the international slave trade for at least two decades. Though national politics paid heed to such regionally defined issues, there was hardly any sense that the South was seriously at odds with the nation and less still that the South and southerners did not "belong" in the new American nation.

All that would change. By the time of the secession crisis in 1860 people on both sides of the sectional chasm had come to believe not only that that there was a North and South but that these were two different and incompatible societies. The South acted on that belief by trying to withdraw from the nation, start its own nation, and protect its differences. The North went to war to keep the Union together, then destroy slavery, the basis for the sectional differences, and then reconstruct the South in the northern image.

THE OTHER ITALY

Southern Italy, the former Bourbon Kingdom of Naples and Sicily, joined the new state under entirely different circumstances. Isolated from others on the Italian peninsula and exposed to a series of invasions and conquests by foreign powers, the South had come from a very different historical realm when it joined Italy in 1860. Most northerners saw the Mezzogiorno as a backward, barbarous region enslaved by feudal society and superstitious religion. The annexation of the South aroused a mix of nationalist optimism at forging L'Italia Unità and xenophobic horror at mixing with alien peoples, and this was a reaction felt in different ways both North and South.

Prime Minister Cavour was a great admirer of Britain, France, and northern Europe. He had never been south of Florence, where he once spent a few restless days.[2] His ignorance of what northerners called "Lower Italy" was astonishing. He believed, for example, that the people of Naples spoke Arabic as a legacy of African invasions. No wonder Cavour was horrified to learn in May 1860 that Garibaldi and a volunteer army of one thousand Italians, mostly from the North, were planning to carry the Risorgimento south. They planned to invade Sicily, ally with peasant uprisings there, and liberate the South from the rule of Ferdinand II, the Bourbon king.

Garibaldi struck out on his expedition to Sicily as much to spite Cavour and the Piedmont conservatives as from any conviction that southerners belonged in some common nation. He was infuriated by Cavour's secret agreement with Napoleon III to give his native land, Nice, to France in exchange for French aid in throwing the Austrians out of Lombardy. Now Garibaldi went south to reclaim the Risorgimento as a popular movement that would embrace all Italians, even if southerners did not think of themselves as Italian. The northerners with Garibaldi saw themselves liberating their fratelli d'Italia from the yokes of despotism and superstition. One of Garibaldi's soldiers wrote in his diary as the expedition set sail for Marsala: "So two ships with the names of two free provinces, Piedmont and Lombardy, are sailing to bring liberty to two slave provinces" (referring to Sicily and Naples).[3] Like their American counterparts behind Generals Ulysses S. Grant and William T. Sherman, the Garabaldini went south on a mission to liberate an enslaved people.

In Sicily Garibaldi's soldiers were astonished to find peasants in bare feet, dressed in goatskins, bowing and kissing hands, feudal acts of humility they now bestowed upon their saviors from the North. These peasants had no idea of the Italian Risorgimento, nor of Italy for that matter. As Garibaldi and his Thousand marched across Sicily they held up one finger to signify "one Italy" and shouted, "Viva L'Italia." Many Sicilians had it in their minds that Garibaldi was the king and that "La Talia" was the name of his queen. For their part, most northerners were equally ignorant of the southern reaches of the peninsula they came to unite with Italy. There was remarkably little travel and commerce between northern and southern portions of the peninsula and almost no effort to bridge the gulf of mutual ignorance between the two. The nationalists from the North were nonetheless optimistic. Early notions of the South by liberal democrats who came with Garibaldi saw it as a land and people enslaved by despotism and the church. The Bourbons, the landlords, and the church had imposed a yoke of tyranny and superstition for generations on the South. Once lifted, the South would rise. Sicilians and Neapolitans would fully become fratelli d'Italia, full members in the new Italian family.

Southern peasants wanted that yoke lifted as well, and they welcomed Garibaldi and his soldiers as liberators, allies in a war against the landlords and the church. One of Garibaldi's men recorded the disparity between the men in red shirts who wanted to liberate and unify Italy and peasants in bare feet who wanted social revolution. "We want to make one great people," he told a radical priest in Sicily. "You mean, one territory," the priest responded;

"as far as the people are concerned, one or many, they are bound to suffer and they go on suffering and I have not heard that you want to make them happy." "What do you want then?" he asked the priest. "War! We want war, not against the Bourbons only, but against all oppressors, great and small, who are not only at court but in every city, in every hamlet."[4]

Garibaldi may have sympathized with the priest, for he held strong liberal convictions and despised the old regime alliance of feudal landlords and the clergy. But he had become convinced that national unity could be achieved only under the aegis of Piedmont and the Savoy monarchy, and he dared do nothing to invite their opposition. To secure their support he made sure that the invasion of Sicily did not turn into a state-sponsored revolution against the big landlords and the church. Indeed, when peasants rose up against their landlords in Bronte, Garibaldi's officers ordered the leaders executed by firing squad. This act presaged the continuity of the old regime of large landholders and an emiserated peasantry of sharecroppers with the Mafia and other criminal organizations emerging as intermediaries. It was these oppressive conditions that set the stage for the great migration of Italian peasants out of the South to the Americas. In Italy, as in the United States, reconstruction and radical social reform in each South were subordinated to the paramount goal of national unity.

The view from the north of Italy saw the South as a "paradise inhabited by the devil," a land blessed by nature with warm climate and abundant crops but cursed by a people who were barbaric, anarchistic, and morally flawed, a people who could be ruled only by force.[5] "We have acquired a very bad country," one northerner wrote from the South after unification, "but it seems impossible that in a place where nature has done so much for the land, it has not generated another people."[6] "What can you possibly build out of stuff like this!" one governor of Naples wrote in 1860. "If only our accursed civilisation did not forbid floggings, cutting out peoples' tongues, and noyades. Then something would happen."[7] To many it seemed the southern people they had "acquired" were something other than Italy, *altro che Italia*. Conquered and occupied by Greeks, Arabs, and others who were alien to Christian civilization and isolated from it for so long, the South of Italy was frequently compared to Africa. "What barbarism! Some Italy!" wrote one government official to Cavour. "This is Africa: the Bedouin are the flower of civil virtue compared to these peasants."[8] "Here we are amongst a population which, although in Italy and born Italian, seems to belong to the primitive tribes of Africa," wrote another northerner.[9]

The early impressions of this "other Italy" exaggerated the alien qualities of the South and reassured northern Italians of their own European affinities. Africa began below Rome. "Christ stopped at Eboli," according to one local expression. Above "lower Italy" was a Christian, European civilization; below it existed something else indeed. The idea of a civilized North and a barbaric South took on important meaning for the way in which the former would govern the latter.

A recurrent theme in much of the early northern impressions of the South was the notion of inherent moral flaws in the people, cultural flaws perhaps but tantamount to racial traits that placed southerners beyond any hope of reform. "Oh! That Naples, how it is fatal to Italy! Corrupt country, vile, devoid of that virtue of service that marks Piedmont, of which that undefeated wisdom that distinguishes central Italy and Tuscany especially."[10] "Believe me," wrote one Piedmont official to Massimo d'Azeglio from Naples in 1861, "it is not us who profit from union, but it is these unfortunate people without morals, without courage, without knowledge."[11]

D'Azeglio, so famously quoted about the need to "make Italians," had adamantly opposed unification with the South and warned that it would bring an alien people and infectious moral diseases into the new Italian state. "In every way the fusion with the Neapolitans makes me afraid," he wrote; "it is like putting yourself to bed with a small pox patient." A year later, he employed another medical metaphor describing Naples as "an ulcer that gnaws at us." "In the North patriotism dominates, in the South interests," another distraught official from Piedmont wrote; "there sacrifice is spontaneous, here it works for egoism; in the North one reflects, here in the South one skips about; . . . in high Italy one knows the political life, in the lower one it is ignored absolutely; above, is civil education, below public corruption."[12] The flaws of "lower Italy" now threatened to debase all of Italy.

A FORCED UNION

The triumph of Garibaldi's southern campaign, it seemed, had embraced within the frontiers of the new Italian nation a people that did not belong and could be neither assimilated into the national family nor subordinated to its rule. "And who are we?" asked one worried northern Italian. "A Nation and not a Nation: united and disunited: drawn, sooner or later into a long and terrible war."[13] Indeed, a long and terrible war was required before the South was finally brought under effective control of the Italian state. In what remains one of the darkest episodes in modern Italian history, a prolonged war between the Italian army and southern outlaws took place in the South throughout the 1860s. The so-called Brigands War witnessed more men killed than in all the wars for independence combined. At its peak, more than two-thirds of the Italian army was deployed in the South to put down domestic unrest. One former Bourbon official reported that Piedmontese troops were treating southerners "not as people fighting for their independence, but as slaves who have revolted against their masters."[14]

John Dickie's book *Darkest Italy* examines how the stereotype of the brigand was employed to create in these southern rebels the antithesis of the modern Italian national ideal, embodied in

the Italian army. It became a war between Italian civilization and
southern barbarism. Reports of brigands drinking blood from the
skulls of their enemy, crucifying enemies, and committing horrible tortures and mutilations became stock items in the propaganda war against the rebels. As part of the army's strategy of
debasing the brigands in the eyes of the nation and demoralizing
them, it adopted a practice of photographing the corpses of slain
brigand leaders. Some photographs were copied in engravings and
published widely in the popular press. In one an Italian soldier
holds up the head of the bandit Nicola Napolitano by his hair;
his corpse is propped up in a chair, clearly posed for the occasion,
while his tongue hangs out of his mouth in a grotesque manner.
Later, studies of brigand physical features would be employed by
the criminologist Cesare Lombroso (who worked as a doctor in
Calabria during the war) to prove the hereditary characteristics
of criminal types. Within the framework of this discourse, the
objective of the state was to repress and destroy the most violent
aspects of southern barbarism, not to reform the region. It was
out of this early, violent conflict with the South that the Italian
Southern Question took form in the 1870s.

The campaign against the rebellious Italian South had begun
in August 1861 when d'Azeglio wrote: "In Naples we drove out a
king in order to establish a government based on universal consent.
But we need sixty battalions to hold southern Italy down, and even
they seem inadequate. What with brigands and nonbrigands, it is
notorious that nobody wants us there." We "have no right to use
guns on them," he went on, unless the new Italian state wants to
be like the Bourbon despots it deposed.[15]

SLAVERY AND THE SOUTHERN PROBLEM

Despite their many important differences, the Italian Brigands
War and the American Civil War were parallel struggles of young

nations to subdue rebellious provinces. Quite unlike the Italian South, the American South had joined the Union as a privileged partner. Though signs of regional conflict of interest were evident in the debates over the Constitution, it was not until the 1830s that the antislavery movement began to sharpen regional consciousness. By the late 1840s sectional antagonism had become sufficiently defined and problematic that people could talk about North and South as though they were coherent, identifiable places with conflicting interests and values. We need not retrace the long road that led from there to secession and Civil War to deal with the basic questions: How did the South come to be seen—from both sides of the divide—as a place and a people that did not belong in the American national community? How did northerners and southerners begin to imagine one another as incompatible enemies?

The turn toward sectional conflict pivoted on the issue of slavery, but the antislavery movement did not lead immediately to condemnation of the South. Indeed, antislavery sentiment was not a sectional issue at all in its earliest stages. Most Americans blamed the British for introducing slavery to America, and Thomas Jefferson's early draft of the Declaration of Independence even listed this as one of the "long train of abuses" that justified revolution. The American Colonization Society began in 1817 with the morally neutral idea that slavery was a racial problem; the task was to find practical ways to remove the freed slave from the midst of a white man's republic. Even when the radical movement for immediate abolition sprang up after 1830, it condemned slavery as a national and not specifically a southern sin. Many abolitionists pointed out that the North was culpable by its involvement in the slave trade and its profit from the cotton economy. But more than that, Horace Bushnell argued, northerners "have a common character with the South, we are one nation. . . . A man's right hand cannot be a thief's and his left an honest man's."[16]

The denunciation of slavery as a national sin required a condemnation of the evils slavery caused, not only those affecting the slave but more important those afflicting whites. That, in turn, led antislavery advocates to evaluate the South as the degraded and perverted product of the institution of slavery. Slavery, this argument went, was the social foundation for an aristocracy whose power over slaves and over the entire society corrupted American ideals of equality and democracy. Beneath the slaveholding aristocracy, the South's critics saw a mass of "poor whites" oppressed by poverty, illiteracy, and lack of opportunity. Slavery was at the root of a general pattern of economic and social backwardness. Census statistics and travel accounts measured the lack of adequate transportation, the absence of towns and cities, the dearth of industry, and the poverty and ignorance of the masses. Slavery was an inherently inefficient system of labor, its northern critics charged, and reliance on slave labor discouraged technological innovation, industrialization, and overall improvement. The ill effects of slavery were also seen in moral terms. The power slavery gave to one human being over others had fostered cruelty, violence, and sexual depravity.

Against this sordid antislavery image of an aristocratic, backward, and barbarous South was the northern model of what America ought to be. America was meant to be a democratic, liberal society based on the ideals of equality and liberty, the essence of which was free labor. Contrasting the ideal America and the southern "other," there developed what Susan-Mary Grant calls "northern nationalism" by which the North came to see itself as the repository of national ideals and the South its perversions. The "image of the blighted South," Grant writes, "often said more about the North's self-image than it did about the reality of the South." It was a construction of myth and history that distorted the reality of both regions. But such distortions were essential to nationalism; as Ernest Renan explained, "Historical error is a crucial factor in the creation of a nation."[17]

In this case, such distortions also became a crucial factor in the division of a nation. Before the Mexican War (1845–48) the northern condemnation of the South as a backward, aristocratic, and un-American society might have persisted as harmless regional prejudice of the type commonly found even in smaller and more homogeneous nations. But slavery was to become a national problem beginning in the late 1840s. The war with Mexico suddenly opened a new empire for slavery. Between the Mexican War and the rise of the Republican Party in 1854, antislavery forces reformulated the condemnation of "the South as a victim of slavery" into a conspiracy theory that envisioned the "Slave Power" threatening the entire republic.

After the South was characterized as a distinctive society perverted by slavery, the notion of a Slave Power plotting to expand its influence in the national government to protect and expand slavery became believable. Slavery and the society it fostered might include several new states carved out of Texas and the vast new territory wrested from Mexico. Each new state brought two more senators and several congressmen to defend the Slave Power. The Kansas-Nebraska Act of 1854 opened a large western territory to slavery by popular vote, then the invasion of proslavery "border ruffians" from Missouri and a violent civil war in "Bleeding Kansas" demonstrated the Slave Power's will to expand. Then the southern-dominated U.S. Supreme Court's Dred Scott decision ruled that Congress had no right to restrict slave owners from taking their property into any state or territory. It revealed to Republicans that the Slave Power intended to make all of America safe for slavery. The Republican Party arose in reaction to this expansionary plan. Out of the materials assembled by the antislavery campaign the Republicans pulled together a powerful critique of slavery and the evil society that was built on it. To this was added the idea of an expanding and seditious Slave Power that was on a course to destroy the nation.[18]

No one put this concept more succinctly than Abraham Lincoln in his House Divided speech:

> This government cannot endure permanently half slave and half free. . . . It will become all one thing, or all the other. Either the opponents of slavery will arrest the further spread of it, and place it where the public mind shall rest in the belief that it is in the course of ultimate extinction, or its advocates will push it forward till it shall become alike lawful in all the States, old as well as new, North as well as South.[19]

Central to this view was the idea that slavery and free labor were foundations for two distinct social systems that could not coexist. Of course, they did coexist in the South, where by 1860 two-thirds of the population was free and three-quarters of the free population owned no slaves. But for Republicans the South was exactly the model of an aristocratic, backward, immoral society that America stood in danger of becoming should they fail to stop the Slave Power conspiracy. According to Republican ideology, the aims of the Slave Power conspiracy began with the expansion of slavery through imperialist conquest abroad and legal political conquest within. Another risk was the reopening of the international slave trade to bring in more Africans. Opponents of the Slave Power went so far as to argue that its ultimate aim was to reduce white laborers North and South to some form of slavery. Through such arguments the antislavery appeal moved beyond moral concerns for African victims or for the South as a society corrupted by slavery. The ultimate threat the Slave Power posed, in the eyes of Republicans, was to undermine the whole American experiment in freedom.[20]

FROM SEPARATISM TO NATIONALISM

The northern evolution from antislavery to anti-South to anti–Slave Power conspiracy had its parallel in the growth of southern sectionalism and the emergence of a separatist movement. Before 1850, none surpassed white southerners in their patriotism toward America, especially in time of war. At no time was this more evident than in the celebrations of the Union's birthday.

On the Fourth of July 1844, the citizens of Oxford, Mississippi, organized a public day of celebration, prayer, speeches, and patriotic ritual to celebrate their membership in the Union. They began the day in church with a prayer meeting. Then in a long procession, with six to eight hundred people, including one hundred ladies, they marched to a barbecue. Among the toasts they raised their glasses to that day the most vehement were those that celebrated the Union and denounced any who might threaten its integrity. "Our Federal Union—Formed into a perfect compact and hearty body by mutual concession and compromise. . . . Palsied be the heart and withered the hand that shall contemplate its destruction." Another saluted "Our Union.—United by the purest blood of patriotism; preserved by the hand of God, and undivided devotion of a free people.—May the execrations of Heaven fall upon him who would sacrilegiously attempt to dissolve the compact."[21]

Even as they approached the brink of secession from the Union, southerners were celebrating its birth each Fourth of July. But now American patriotism was tempered by fears that "southern rights" within the Union were imperiled by northern abolitionists. By the time Mississippi congressman Lucius Quintus Cinninatus Lamar gave his maiden speech in Congress in 1858 the tension between loyalty to the South and the Union was acute: "Others may boast of their . . . love of this Union. With me, I confess that the promotion of Southern interests is second in importance only to the preservation of Southern honor."[22] A year later he saw southern rights imperiled by the growth of antislavery agitation, and he announced: "I war upon your government, I am against it. I raise then the banner of secession, and I will fight under it as long as the blood flows and ebbs in my veins."[23] American patriots were becoming south-

ern separatists and American nationalism was being supplanted
by southern nationalism—or was it? What was the rationale for
southern separatism? What was the basis for Confederate nationalism? On what did southerners stake their claim for nationhood
before the world and their own citizens?

Even before the war began there were arguments that some form
of primordial, ethnic differences separated North and South. The
historian James McPherson has argued that southerners invented a
brand of ethnic nationalism from the Puritan-Cavalier thesis. This
"central myth of Southern ethnic nationalism," he argues, drew
upon "the idea that Southern whites . . . were descended from the
English Cavaliers of the seventeenth century . . . while Yankees
were descended from the 'Saxon churls' by way of the seventeenth-
century Puritans." This separate origins myth was embraced by
northerners who sought to explain the aristocratic and backward
nature of the South but also by those southerners proud to claim
an aristocratic Cavalier heritage.[24]

Confederate leaders also identified their cause with those of
other nationalist struggles, some of them rooted in primordial conflicts between different ethnic and religious groups. The Scottish
struggle against the English was a popular inspiration for southerners, and Sir Walter Scott's novels became staple campfire reading
among Confederate soldiers. More recent struggles by the Greeks
for independence from the Turks and, ironically, the Italians to
oust the Bourbons from Sicily and Naples served as inspiration for
a Confederate nation that wanted to see itself part of the historic
struggle for national freedom.[25]

No doubt these analogies with other national independence
movements and the stereotypes of Cavalier and Yankee, southern
aristocrat and northern capitalist, all had their role in enabling
the combatants to imagine one another as enemies. Ethnic and
regional stereotypes gave people a language with which to describe
regional differences. "I fear Northerner and Southerner are aliens,"

New Yorker George Templeton Strong wrote in his diary in 1860, "not merely in social and political arrangements, but in mental and moral constitution. We differ like Celt and Anglo-Saxon."[26]

The ethnic theory of separate Cavalier and Puritan origins and the cultural argument that North and South had fundamentally different values and ways of life continued long after the war to appeal to those seeking an explanation for the "irrepressible conflict." But at the time of that conflict, these ideas acted as superficial and supplemental justifications for conflicts that were clearly rooted in more immediate political, economic, and racial concerns. Logically it made little sense for northerners to embrace such primordial explanations. Whatever northerners thought about the South and its cultural differences, they were sacrificing the blood and treasure of the nation to keep the South in the Union. The preferred explanation among Republicans, as I argued above, was that southern differences stemmed from slavery and the remedy was abolition and reconstruction.

Confederate leaders made their strongest case for separation to the world and to their own people not on ethnic or cultural differences but on principles, interests, and rights. Using the same Lockean logic of the American Revolution, they argued that they had joined a federation of sovereign states that now had abused their rights. The victory of a sectional party hostile to the South gave them no choice but to secede. "Our position is thoroughly identified with the institution of slavery," L. Q. C. Lamar wrote in Mississippi's declaration of causes for secession; "a blow at slavery is a blow at commerce and civilization." The Mississippi declaration, borrowing Jefferson's language, submitted a long "train of abuses" proving the conspiracy against slavery. "We must either submit to degradation, and to the loss of property worth four billions of money, or we must secede from the Union framed by our fathers, to secure this as well as every other species of property. For far less cause than this, our fathers separated from the Crown of

England."[27] Each state's declaration of secession reveals a similar emphasis on political issues and material interests, not cultural or ethnic differences between the northern and southern people.[28]

There was a strong racial basis for southern nationhood founded on the principle of white supremacy with slavery as a means of racial subordination. Beneath the legal arguments for the right to secede and the political arguments for the necessity to secede were fundamental racial concerns that provided a motive for southern separatism. More was at stake than the property rights of slave owners, for slavery was the bulwark of a larger system of white supremacy. No one put this more clearly than Alexander Stephens, vice-president of the Confederacy, when he said: "Our new government is founded upon exactly the opposite idea" of human equality; "its foundations are laid, its corner-stone rests upon the great truth, that the negro is not equal to the white man; that slavery—subordination to the superior race—is his natural and normal condition." "With us," Stephens went on, "all of the white race, however high or low, rich or poor, are equal in the eye of the law."[29] Slavery was the guarantor of white supremacy, and above the color line whites shared an equality as members of the same national community. Whiteness, rather than any specific ethnic identity, was a primary source of Confederate national solidarity.

White southerners had reason to see their northern enemy's campaign against slavery as dangerous to the security of this cornerstone of white supremacy. Initially the antislavery movement undertook peaceful "moral suasion" through pamphlets, petitions, and political campaigns. By the late 1850s, however, southerners saw abolitionism as a direct-action terrorist movement that aimed at inciting slaves to rebel against their masters and inflict violence on all whites. John Brown's terrifying raid at Harpers Ferry in 1859 only confirmed long-standing fears. Well before that, southern newspapers reported themselves besieged by subversive abolitionist agents and slave conspiracies. This took the issue well beyond the

simple material interests in protecting slave property, for abolitionist terrorism portended general racial chaos. White southerners,
rich and poor, could see themselves threatened by abolitionists
invading from without and murderous slaves rising from below.
Local communities organized armed vigilance committees and
reported suspicious behavior through the local press.

In the shadow of abolitionist terror any dissent from the southern
rights hard line might be seen as subversive. The voice of Union and
compromise was silenced as the white South closed ranks against
abolitionism. "It was now dangerous to utter a word in favour of
the Union," one stubborn opponent of secession in Mississippi reported.[30] White solidarity "united by a sense of terrible danger,"
not Cavalier or Celtic ethnic origins, was what provided the racial
basis for an emerging nationalist movement.[31]

After the war began and after Lincoln issued the Emancipation
Proclamation the predictions of northern aggression and racial upheaval took on a new validity. Invading Union soldiers actively encouraged slaves to rebel or abandon their masters, and blacks were
recruited to serve in the Union army. Now the South's nightmare
became reality: Union soldiers, like John Brown in multitudes,
inciting slave rebellion and slaves armed and wearing the enemy
uniform, empowered to destroy their masters' world.

The racial motivation for separation was not the same as a primordial argument for white southerners as a separate people distinct from and incompatible with those of the North. The birth
of the Confederate nation was like that of the United States; it
involved breaking away from a people with whom they shared a
common tradition of law, language, and religion. Economically
both sections were integrally involved in the same capitalist industrial society, the cotton planters supplying its most vital raw material. The Northeast had experienced more urban and industrial
development than either the South or West, but the entire country
was still overwhelmingly rural and agricultural. The South had

to make its case as a nation on principle rather than on essential differences as a people.

The essence of Confederate nationalism was forged out of the same materials that went into the American nation they were repudiating. The Confederates appropriated the very symbols and language of American nationalism. George Washington, the father of the country they were leaving, became the stepfather of the country they were inventing. His image was on the seal of the Confederacy. The Confederate president, Jefferson Davis, was inaugurated in Richmond in 1862 at the base of Washington's statue and on his birthday. The Confederate States of America adopted the U.S. Constitution almost verbatim and imitated most of its laws. In these and other ways they adopted American nationalism as their own and argued that they were loyal to the original ideals of the American Revolution; it was their northern enemies who had betrayed it. In American nationalism they had a ready-made justification for their separatist revolt.[32] What they did not have was a fully separate national identity.

The borrowing of American nationalism also softened what may have been the strongest source of national solidarity in a war for independence: hatred of a common enemy. Confederate nationalism, wrote David Potter, "was born of resentment and not of a sense of separate cultural identity."[33] The abolitionist condemnation of the South as a backward, immoral, violent society may not have been as accepted in the North as it was resented in the South. The antislavery crusade condemned the sin and the sinner when it denounced slavery as a cruel institution that left families torn asunder and women ravaged. Southerners attending northern colleges found themselves harassed by northern students. Northern antislavery politicians made ad hominem attacks on their southern opponents. News of Preston Brooks caning Charles Sumner on the floor of the U.S. Senate for insulting his relative was greeted with wild enthusiasm in the South. It took a woman like Mary Chesnut to fully understand the emotions that drove the South to separate: "We separated," she wrote in her diary, "because of incompatibility of temper; we are divorced, North from South, because we have hated each other so."[34] Perhaps, but she might have added, because, like long-married couples, they had also been bound so long by interest and affection and by a common history as a nation; only hatred could have driven them to secession and war.

The strongest stimulus to Confederate nationalism might have been the invading enemy that threatened the safety and prosperity of its citizens. As the Union army drove deep into the Confederacy in the West and as Lincoln transformed the war into a struggle over slavery, the northern threat to southern security took on an undeniable reality. Hatred of a common enemy can provide powerful sources of national feeling, as the modern world knows all too well. Liah Greenfeld tells us that resentment, "suppressed feelings of envy and hatred," often festers in a nation that is objectively inferior or subordinate to another. Such feelings had served as a major source of national identity for the French against the English.[35] Resentment and hatred were perhaps necessary ingredients for nationalism but in themselves not always sufficient. Modern wars and the atrocities and losses that accompany them generate their own motives for hating an enemy. Whether the American Civil War was the first genuine total war is debatable, but it inflicted terrific punishment on the southern home front to say nothing of its military.

Even children learned to hate the enemy. One Confederate schoolbook asked: "If one Confederate soldier kills 90 Yankees, how many can 10 Confederate soldiers kill?"[36] This schoolbook lesson was but one of a multitude of such efforts the new Confederate nation hastily activated in an effort to create a new national identity or transform the old one. New flags, uniforms, cockades, songs, and other outward symbols of loyalty to the independence movement were quickly rolled out to signify national loyalty. The nascent culture of Confederate nationalism was publicly performed on such occasions as flag presentation ceremonies to the men going off to war. Young women, dressed in virginal white dresses, with sashes emblazoned with the name of each seceded state, presented company battle flags to the young men going to war to protect them. The North, one Mississippi belle told the soldiers before her, "may attempt to invade our land and lay waste our fields, in order to constrain us to submit to degradation. When that hour comes, if come it should, we rely upon your strong arms and unquailing hearts to defend our rights, protect the mothers, shield the honor of the maidens of the land, and give security and peace to our fire-sides."[37] Through such rituals Confederate nationalism integrated the identities men and women had as members of families and communities with the larger cause of southern independence. There were military drills and parades on town squares and countless other ceremonies designed to weld local to national loyalties, to give young men something to fight for and their families a cause worthy of their sacrifice. Young men would go off to fight and die for their families and for the extended kinship system that was their nation.

DEFEAT AND NATIONALISM

Did the Confederacy die for want of nationalism? Throughout the war signs of serious morale problems were evident in desertion, draft dodging, pro-Union opposition, trading with the enemy, and peace movements. Men felt torn between their obligations to feed and protect their families and to serve and defend their collective family, the nation that had called them to arms. The widespread disloyalty of slaves who fled to the Union army was another major cause of demoralization. The protests of women against the deprivations of war, food riots, and other signs of discontent provide further evidence of vacillating loyalties. The commitment to states' rights also compromised national solidarity.[38]

These signs of disloyalty and weak nationalism may be better understood as products than causes of military defeat.[39] There were similar signs of wavering nationalism and vacillating loyalties in the North. The historian John Murrin, commenting on the frailty of American national identity during the Revolution, argues that "its social roots were much weaker than those that brought forth the Confederate States of America in 1861, and yet the Confederacy was successfully crushed by military force."[40] It took four years of hard fighting before the South succumbed to what by most measures was a vastly superior adversary. If nations create nationalism, the Confederate nation was only beginning to construct the elements of a national identity before it was defeated. Nationalism, Drew Faust points out, is always insufficient at the outset because it is contingent on the success of the nation in winning its right to exist.[41]

Though many modern nations, including the United States, were born in separatist movements, such rebellions are usually considered illegitimate—unless they win. David Potter once wrote that treason is never successful "because if it is successful it is not treason."[42] Among linguists, who argue over the difference between a language and a dialect, there is an expression that a language is simply a dialect with an army and navy. It might also be said that a nation is nothing more than a region with an army and navy, and most revolutions for national independence are nothing more than successful secessionist movements. Triumphant separatists write their own national histories while failed rebels sulk as conquered subalterns in the nation they tried to leave or forget they ever wanted out of it. The losers mourn lost causes, fuel resentment, and perhaps wait to fight another day.

Whatever the source and strength of southern nationalism before and during the war, it found new life in defeat. In the Lost Cause white southerners tempered the verdict of the battlefield and the judgment of history with a version of the past that salvaged honor from failure. To recall Ernest Renan's poignant observation, made after his country's loss to Germany in the Franco-Prussian War, "suffering in common unifies more than joy does."[43]

The women of the South, notably the United Daughters of the Confederacy, took up the duties of grieving shared sorrows and guarding the past with patriotic devotion. They reviewed American history textbooks making sure that "the war between the states" was interpreted correctly as one in which "both sides were equally patriotic and both honest defenders of unsolved national questions, and in which neither was in rebellion." They prepared a Confederate Catechism for Children that asked: "How were the slaves treated?" The answer: "With great kindness and care in nearly all cases, a cruel master being rare." The slaves, they also were taught to believe, "were faithful and devoted and were always ready and willing to serve" their masters; during the war they "nobly protected and cared for the wives of soldiers in the field. They were always true and loyal."[44] As Eric Hobsbawm wrote, "Getting its history wrong is part of being a nation."[45]

As women tended to the preservation of the past, white men constructed a postemancipation system of disfranchisement and segregation designed to ensure the subjugation of blacks. The ascendance of the Lost Cause and the new order of white supremacy coincided with the reconciliation between North and South toward the end of the nineteenth century. Southern nationalism again fused with American nationalism and imagined enemies lived in peace again. "As the sections reconciled," the historian David Blight writes, "the races divided."[46]

The "essence of a nation," Ernest Renan told us, "is that all individuals have many things in common, and also that they have forgotten many things." "It is good for everyone to know how to forget."[47] America, the "first new nation," depended on its immigrants to forget their hatreds and resentments in the New World they made home. The United States also demonstrated that its brand of civic nationalism could tear a country apart every bit as viciously as primordial nationalism. Now healed, "one nation indivisible" entered the twentieth century reunited in a civic nationalism of shared belief in freedom and equality, which rested uncomfortably on a form of white nationalism that left black Americans not fully belonging. For their part, black Americans held on tenaciously to the citizenship they had won, endured its abuses, and, in time, reasserted their claim to full membership in the American national community. Meanwhile, most Americans were learning "how to forget"—not the war, which became a curiously celebrated episode in the nation's history but the central issues of slavery and race that had caused it.

ITALY'S SOUTHERN QUESTION REDUX

The Italian Southern Question did not find an answer following the long and bloody Brigands War. Instead a series of government reports and essays dwelled on what they saw as the intractable problems of southern poverty and the racial inferiority and criminal propensities of southern people, particularly the Mafia.[48] Millions of the southern peasantry sought escape as immigrants to North and South America. Following World War II Italy experienced a Great Migration not unlike that of the United States; millions of southern peasants moved north to Turin and other industrial centers. The postwar "Italian Miracle" of industrial development depended to no small degree on cheap, available southern migrant labor, but their arrival in the North only intensified regional prejudice. Northerners commonly referred to the southern migrants as *terrone* (roughly translated as "dirt") and blamed them for most of the social problems that attended rapid urban and industrial growth.

Even as consciousness of regional differences sharpened, there was little talk of separation. Following World War II, inspired by the liberation of their land by the American GIs, Sicilians mounted a short-lived movement to secede from Italy and join the United States as the forty-ninth state. The United States government was more concerned that Italy, particularly its impoverished South, would ally with the communists, and it helped fund a massive program to aid economic development of the South. Modeled after the Tennessee Valley Authority that brought electric power to the American South, this program fell under the control of corrupt politicians and their Mafia allies. Following the Cold War the corruption and futility of this program in particular fueled the rise of the northern separatist movement.

Overshadowing these internal divisions in Italy and Western Europe was the hostile reaction to African, Middle Eastern, Eastern European, and other "extra-communitarian" immigrants who entered Europe seeking work.[49] Nativist political movements in nearly every Western European country mobilized those reactionary elements who wanted to preserve their national heritage by excluding immigrants or restricting their rights. The Americanization of Europe was nowhere more evident than in this backlash toward immigrants whose labor was desperately needed but whose skin color, religion, and culture threatened national homogeneity. The incursion of these outsiders challenged the very idea of nationhood imagined to rest on common origin, culture, and history. To an American eye, it all seemed very familiar.

5

Nationalism Reconsidered

The United States of America, instead of being exceptional, in many ways predicted the experience of European nations in the twentieth century. America was a vast container into which poured a multitude of immigrant cultures, languages, and religions. Becoming American called on newcomers to speak English and adopt new behaviors if they wanted to achieve individual success, but it did not demand that immigrants give up ethnic, religious, and other identities. The burdens of nationalism, whether official or popular, rested lightly on a vast, decentralized society. America allowed tremendous room for a variety of ethnic, regional, and other alternative identities to flourish under the national umbrella. Jews and Mormons, Cajuns and Texans, Asians and African Americans, liberals and conservatives could nurture their own identities without having to repudiate the American one in which they nested.

The new nation of Italy encased a multitude of long-standing provincial cultures whose language, customs, and identities persisted long after Italy was made. From its inception as a state, Italy's national identity has coexisted with a powerful tradition of *campanilismo*, that attachment to the local community and family that has somehow survived massive migration and industrialization. Until the television age, when dubbed Hollywood productions introduced standard Italian into the home, local dialects had endured in everyday use, just as regional food and wine remain rooted to specific locales. In Italy people commonly refer to one another by their regional identity as Sicilians, Piedmontese, Sardinians, Romans, or Venitians. They become Italians outside Italy.

Ever since Italy was born, Italian intellectuals have been wringing their hands over the lack of strong national identity, but the Northern League and its bellicose call for separation has provoked a new outpouring of concern. Books with titles such as *La morte della patria* (The death of the motherland), *Italiani senza Italia* (Italians without Italy), and *Il Risorgimento imperfetto* (The imperfect Risorgimento) echo the same anguished cry Ferdinando Martini attributed to Massimo d'Azeglio a century earlier: "We must make Italians."[1] Meanwhile, Italians continue embracing their local attachments to family and community and, for the most part, they reject Northern League nationalism along with the official Italian nationalism.

Intellectuals elsewhere generally worry about the excesses, not the weakness, of nationalism in the world. The problem with nationalism, in their view, is not its spurious but generally inoffensive claims to community and tradition. Ultimately, all communities are imagined, and all traditions have their origin in human invention. If the justification for nations rests on a false sense of common characteristics or a distorted history, so does the rationalization for most other human groups that lay claim on their members' loyalty and espouse some common cause. Labor unions, political parties, and protest movements all invite their followers to join an imagined community of interest and sentiment. Indeed, extended kinship groups are imaginary communities, as anyone who has attended a large family reunion can attest.

The objection to nationalism comes not from its relatively harmless pretensions to shared origin or timeless continuity but from intolerant tribalism and claims of superiority that lead to brutal treatment of dissidents within and violent aggression against outsiders. If the worst atrocities carried out by dictators, warlords, and football hooligans in the name of nationalism are sometimes unfairly laid at the doorstep of nationalism, it is because we have come to associate it with the bad company it has been keeping of late.[2]

Should nationalism be understood only as an atavistic force that divides people, its power to unite and transcend those divisions will remain obscure. If we see the alternative to a world of nations as a global community of diverse peoples coexisting without fixed national identities or political borders, then nationalism seems an obsolete residue of an old world—something like those walled cities of the premodern world that amaze tourists. However, when we see the alternative to nationalism in the former Yugoslavia as brutal repression of dissident minorities, internecine wars, and ethnic cleansing, we might see nationalism as something worth reconsidering.

In the Old and New Worlds new forms of economic and political configurations are beginning to supersede the nation-state of old. The North Atlantic Treaty Organization (NATO) created a supranational military agency, one activated recently to douse the flames of ethnonationalism in Eastern Europe. The North American Free Trade Agreement initiated a supranational economic market by phasing out tariffs between Canada, the United States, and Mexico.

Europe is undergoing the most radical departure from traditional notions of nationhood. No place has endured more bloody international strife during the last century. For that reason, and in response to the American challenge, since 1946 Europe has been moving toward what Winston Churchill envisioned as a "United States of Europe." A European federation had been Giuseppe Mazzini's dream a century earlier. Europe, he envisioned in 1847, would become "one vast market . . . marching by the common consent of her populations towards a new era of union . . . all contributing to one work, whose fruits are to enlarge and strengthen the life of all."[3] Now, what has been only a geographic expression is becoming something comparable to states in a federal system. In the European Union members will enjoy free trade and migration across the old national borders. National currencies, one of the everyday reminders of national identity, are about to be subsumed by the Euro.

Much more is involved than economic integration. Along with the flow of goods and the virtual erasure of national frontiers are myriad European Union standards that affect everything from national debt to public access for the disabled. If national currencies and passports are rendered irrelevant in the new European Union, how will the identities of British, French, Italian, and the rest reconcile with an ascending European identity?

In Britain the debate over joining a larger federal nation they call simply "Europe" coincides with the devolution into smaller nations of the United Kingdom. English conservatives embrace British nationalism and decry Scottish independence in the same breath they denounce the loss of British independence to Europe. Opposing this fortress island mentality, the English scholar Timothy Garton Ash answers that "Europe and federalism could be the only way to save Britain. . . . The federal system, tailor-made for multiple identities, is the way forward for Britain, this mysterious nation made of four nations."[4]

Most Italians were proud and eager to become part of the European Union, as though it validated an overdue respect for one of the world's leading industrial powers and offset the country's equally deserved reputation for political volatility. For many Italians becoming part of Europe was something that galvanized rather than diminished national identity and pride.

Italy's northern separatists, in contrast, applauded the new European Union as the precursor to the devolution of united Italy. Eventually, the Northern League proclaimed, the "federation of Regions" protected by the European Union will allow the old nation-states of Italy, along with France, Germany, and the United Kingdom, to dissolve into useless historical artifacts.[5] The separatist nationalism of the Northern League embraces the new European nationalism to serve an older form of tribal nationalism. Devoted primarily to defining incompatible differences between "us" and "them," the league's mean brand of nationalism says differences between peoples are real and that they cannot live together in the same political container. Believing makes it so, and conflicts that justify separation within one nation may just as easily be transformed into hostilities across international borders.

One Italian cartoon that circulated clandestinely in the 1990s illustrates "the complete solution to all our problems" with a map showing Italy cut in two by a wide "liberation channel" that divides the peninsula just below Florence. To the south the map shows the "Island of New Africa" and "Mafioso Realm." Each side of the channel has protective barriers two kilometers high, one side electrified, the other armed with laser sensors to keep southern migrants out of the North. The channel is filled with "terrone-eating" sharks and piranhas. North of the channel is Northern Italy and, significantly, a new "Southern Italy" below the Po Valley. Even a separate Northern Italy might need its South.[6]

This imagined division of a nation illustrates the prejudice of one part of a nation toward another but also the absurdity of achieving any genuine solution through secession. President Abraham Lincoln, facing the first major separatist revolt in the modern national era, made exactly this point in his first inaugural address: "Physically speaking, we cannot separate. We cannot remove our respective sections from each other nor build an impassable wall between them. A husband and wife may be divorced and go out of the presence and beyond the reach of each other; but the different parts of our country cannot do this."[7]

The American Union that Lincoln struggled to preserve offered a model of how peoples of remarkable diversity might learn to live together peacefully. It also furnished a horrifying illustration of the price nations pay when they do not learn to live together. For better and for worse, as I maintained at the beginning of this book, America's past would become the future for many nations of the world. As we explore new national structures and identities in the so-called postnational era, we would do well to reconsider the dreams that inspired nationalism in its robust infancy in the Americas and Europe. For whatever better communities we imagine in our future, their achievement may depend on our ability to realize the early promise of nationalism.

NOTES

1. A DEATH AT GETTYSBURG

1. Gage Family Letters, Special Collections, John Williams Library, University of Mississippi, Oxford, Mississippi.

2. J. S. Gage, Gettysburg, Pennsylvania, to Mrs. P. W. Gage, Richland, Holmes County, Mississippi, July 3, 1863, reproduced in James B. Lloyd, *The University of Mississippi: The Formative Years, 1848–1906* (University: University of Mississippi, 1979), 34–35; Maud Morrow Brown, *The University Greys: Company A Eleventh Mississippi Regiment Army of Northern Virginia, 1861–1865* (1940; rpt. Topeka, Kans.: Bonnie Blue Press, 1993), 38–39.

3. My conversation was with Anna Maria Cataldi Palombi, professor of English, Federico II University, Naples, April 1995.

4. Griffin and Doyle, eds., *The South as an American Problem.*

5. Schneider, ed., *Italy's "Southern Question"*; Dickie, *Darkest Italy*; and Griffin and Doyle, eds., *The South as an American Problem*, all examine the role of an internal "other" in sharpening a nation's ideal self-image.

6. Metta Spencer, ed., *Separatism: Democracy and Disintegration* (Lanham, Md.: Rowman & Littlefield, 1998).

7. Tom Nairn, *The Break-up of Britain: Crisis and Neo-Nationalism*, 2d ed. (London: Verso, 1981).

8. See the web sites to *La Padania*, the national newspaper, <http://www.lapadania.com/>, and to the Lega Nord <http://www.leganord.org/>.

9. See the United Nations members list and the complicated explanations of how such new nations as Belarus or Croatia, former regions within member nations, became members in their own right: <http://www.un.org/Overview/unmember.html>.

10. Charles Krauthammer, "Quebec and the Death of Diversity," *Time*, November 13, 1995, 74, quoted in Schwartz, *Last Best Hope*, 10.

11. R. J. M. Blackett, *Divided Hearts: Britain and the American Civil War* (Baton Rouge: Louisiana State University Press, 2001), 14–15.

12. The new Republic of France endured a bloody counterrevolution in the region of Vendèe in 1793, and other new nations experienced resistance to central authority. See Charles Tilly, *The Vendèe: A Sociological Analysis of the Counter-Revolution of 1793* (Cambridge, Mass.: Harvard University Press, 1964). Mexico also faced a bloody separatist revolt in the 1830s, when American settlers broke off from Mexico to establish the Republic of Texas. Brazil faced a separatist revolt in its southern provinces, 1835–1845. The breakup of Gran Colombia in South America occurred without major military conflict. None reached the degree that the Confederate challenge posed to the United States.

2. MAKING NATIONS

1. Charles Sumner, *Are We a Nation?* (New York: New York Young Men's Republican Union, 1867), 5.

2. Walker Conner, "A Nation Is a Nation," *Ethnic and Racial Studies* 1 (1978): 379–88, reprinted in Hutchinson and Smith, *Nationalism*, 36–46.

3. Anderson, *Imagined Communities*.

4. Hobsbawm and Ranger, eds., *Invention of Tradition*; Hobsbawm, *Nations and Nationalism since 1780*.

5. Gellner, *Nations and Nationalism*; see also Gellner, *Encounters with Nationalism*.

6. Clifford Geertz, "The Integrative Revolution: Primordial Sentiments and Civil Politics in the New States," in Geertz, ed., *Old Societies and New States: The Quest for Modernity in Asia and Africa* (New York: Free Press, 1963), 107–13.

7. Anthony D. Smith, "The Nation: Real or Imagined?" in Mortimer, ed., *People, Nation and State*, 39; see also Smith, "The Origins of Nations," *Ethnic and Racial Studies* 12 (1989): 349–56.

8. Suny, "Constructing Primordialism: Old Histories for New Nations,"

presented to the Department of History, Vanderbilt University, March 23, 2001, forthcoming in *Journal of Modern History.* My thanks to Professor Suny for permitting me to quote from his manuscript.

9. Stuart Woolf, "Introduction" to *Nationalism in Europe, 1815 to the Present: A Reader* (London: Routledge, 1996), 4; Federico Chabod, "The Idea of Nation," in Woolf, ed., *Nationalism in Europe, 1815 to the Present,* 124.

10. Wiebe, "Humanizing Nationalism," 81–88.

11. Walker Conner, "When Is a Nation," *Ethnic and Racial Studies* 13 (1992), 38.

12. Anderson, *Imagined Communities,* 46.

13. Pauline Maier, *From Resistance to Revolution: Colonial Radicals and the Development of American Opposition to Britain, 1765–1776* (New York: Norton, 1991).

14. Murrin, "A Roof without Walls: The Dilemma of American National Identity," in Beeman, Botein, and Carter, eds., *Beyond Confederation,* 342; Bernard Bailyn, *The Ideological Origins of the American Revolution* (1967; rpt. Cambridge, Mass.: Harvard University Press, 1992).

15. Breen, "Ideology and Nationalism on the Eve of the American Revolution," 13–39; Douglas Edward Leach, *Roots of Conflict: British Armed Forces and Colonial Americans, 1677–1763* (Chapel Hill: University of North Carolina Press, 1986).

16. Murrin, "Roof without Walls," 340–41.

17. Breen, "Ideology and Nationalism," 13–39.

18. All quotes from Greene, *Intellectual Construction of America,* 162, 164, 173.

19. Robert Gross, *The Minutemen and Their World* (New York: Hill and Wang, 1976).

20. Davis, *Revolutions.*

21. Quoted in Mack Smith, *Mazzini,* 167.

22. William Lloyd Garrison, "Introduction" to *Joseph Mazzini: His Life, Writings, and Political Principles* (New York: Hurd and Houghton, 1872), xvi; Joseph Rossi, *The Image of America in Mazzini's Writings* (Madison: University of Wisconsin Press, 1954), 127.

23. Mack Smith, ed., *Garibaldi,* 69–72.

24. William Caferro, *Mercenary Companies and the Decline of Siena* (Baltimore: Johns Hopkins University Press), 1998.

25. Mack Smith, *Mazzini,* 13.

26. Stendhal, *Rome, Naples and Florence* (1817), quoted in Brendon, ed., *Making of Modern Italy,* 12.

27. The anthem was derived from a poem written by Goffredo Mameli in the American consul in Genoa and was known as "L'Inno di Mameli." The official name of the anthem is "Fratelli d'Italia, l'Italia s'è desta" (Brothers of Italy, Italy has risen). Words and history, including an audio version of the anthem, can be found at the web site of the Istituto Italiano di Cultura, New York: <http://www.italcultny.org/>.

28. Mack Smith, *Mazzini,* 14; Romano Bracalini, *Cattaneo: un federalista per gli Italiani* (Milan: Arnoldo Mondadori, 1995).

29. Riall, *Italian Risorgimento,* 2–3; Antonio Gramsci, *Il Risorgimento* (1949; rpt. Turin: Riuniti, 1979).

30. Herder, *Italy in the Age of the Risorgimento,* 234–35; Duggan, *Concise History of Italy,* 136.

31. Quoted in Brendon, ed., *Making of Modern Italy,* 61.

3. THE DAILY PLEBISCITE

1. Ernest Renan, "What Is a Nation?" in Eley and Suny, eds., *Becoming National,* 53.

2. Wiebe, *"Imagined Communities,* Nationalist Experiences," 33.

3. Ibid., 44.

4. Weber, *Peasants into Frenchmen,* 486.

5. See Silvio Lanaro, "Da Contadini a Italiani."

6. Wiebe, "Humanizing Nationalism," 81–88.

7. Ernest Gellner, *Nationalism* (London: Orion, 1998), 19.

8. Riall, "Hero, Saint or Revolutionary?," 198; Banti, *La Nazione del Risorgimento.*

9. Soldani and Turi, eds., *Fare gli Italiani,* 1:1, quoting Massimo d'Azeglio, *I miei ricordi* 2 vols.(Florence: Barbèra, 1867), 1:6–7. I am grateful to Professor Mia Fuller, who graciously answered my H-Net query

about this quotation. In Italian it is *"pur troppo s'è fatta l'Italia, ma non si fanno gli Italiani."*

10. Quoted in Ronald Marshall, *Massimo d'Azeglio: An Artist in Politics, 1798–1866* (London: Oxford University Press, 1966), 293.

11. Travers, *Celebrating the Fourth,* 70 and passim.

12. Ibid., 72–77.

13. Zelinsky, *Nation into State,* 71.

14. Travers, *Celebrating the Fourth*, 21–22, 49.

15. John F. Berens, *Providence and Patriotism in Early America, 1640–1815* (Charlottesville: University Press of Virginia, 1978), quoted in Zelinsky, *Nation into State*, 71.

16. Zelinsky, *Nation into State*, 71.

17. Travers, *Celebrating the Fourth*, 18, 25, 26, 36, 114–15.

18. Waldstreicher, *In the Midst of Perpetual Fetes,* 9.

19. Don H. Doyle, *The Social Order of a Frontier Community: Jacksonville, Illinois, 1825–70* (Urbana: University of Illinois Press, 1978), 228–32; Don H. Doyle, *Faulkner's County: The Historical Roots of Yoknapatawpha* (Chapel Hill: University of North Carolina Press, 2001), 260, 273.

20. Contrast this tradition with our own time, when the Fourth of July seems to be observed passively by Americans in private backyard barbecues or public fireworks displays viewed silently and mostly from a distance.

21. Duggan, *Concise History of Italy,* 27–28; Bruno Migliorini, *The Italian Language*, abridged, recast, and revised by T. Gwynfor Griffith (London: Faber and Faber, 1984).

22. Porciani, *La Festa della Nazione,* 21, 24, 33–35, quoted on 34.

23. Ibid., 37–38, 169–201.

24. Ibid., 57.

25. *L'Osservatore Cattolico*, 1887, quoted ibid., 206.

26. Wilbur Zelinsky writes: "By general consent among chroniclers of American thought, it is to New England that we must turn for the genesis of the nation-idea, as is true for so many other early advances in technology and in a wide range of social and intellectual activities." Zelinsky, *Nation into State*, 231, 148; Krakau, ed., *The American Nation, National Identity,* 10; Elson, *Guardians of Tradition,* 7.

27. Susan-Mary Grant, *North over South*.

28. Noah Webster, "On the Education of Youth in America," in *A Collection of Essays and Fugitive Writings on Moral, Historical, Political and Literary Subjects* (1790; rpt. Delmar, N.Y.: Scholars' Facsimiles and Reprints, 1977).

29. Ibid.

30. Zelinsky, *Nation into State*, 150, quoting Robert Wood Lynn, "Civil Catechetics in Mid-Victorian America: Some Notes about American Civil Religion, Past and Present," *Religious Education* 68 (1973): 23. See also Dolores P. Sullivan, *William Holmes McGuffey: Schoolmaster to the Nation* (Rutherford, N.J.: Fairleigh Dickinson University Press, 1994); Richard David Mosier, *Making the American Mind: Social and Moral Ideas in the McGuffey Readers* (New York, King's Crown Press, 1947).

31. Greenfeld, *Nationalism*, 445.

32. Elson, *Guardians of Tradition*, 167.

33. Ibid., 102–3.

34. Michael Feldberg, *The Philadelphia Riots of 1844: A Study of Ethnic Conflict* (Westport, Conn.: Greenwood, 1975); Oscar Handlin, *Boston's Immigrants, 1790–1880: A Study in Acculturation* (1949; rpt. Cambridge, Mass.: Harvard University Press, 1991).

35. Porciani, *Festa della Nazione*, 100.

36. Though neither is documented, both quotes are from Adrian Lyttelton, "Building the Italian Nation," paper delivered at conference "The Southern Question: Nationalism and Regionalism in Italy and America," Naples, June 1997.

37. Ibid.

38. De Amicis, *Cuore,* 17.

39. Lyttelton, "Building the Italian Nation"; Davis, *Conflict and Control*, 146–47; Martin Clark, *Modern Italy, 1871–1995*, 2d ed. (London: Longman, 1996), 36–37.

40. Clark, *Modern Italy,* 35–36; C. W. Bennett, *National Education: Italy, France, Germany, England and Wales, Popularly Considered* (Syracuse, N.Y.: N.p., 1878).

41. Davis, *Conflict and Control*, 146–47.

42. Quoted in White, *Progressive Renaissance,* 16–17.

43. Clark, *Modern Italy,* 37.

44. Ibid., 35–36; White, *Progressive Renaissance*, 20. For U.S. literacy figures, see Lawrence A. Cremin, *American Education: The National Experience, 1783–1876* (New York: Harper & Row, 1980), 491.

45. Lyttelton, "Building the Italian Nation."

46. Porciani, *Festa della nazione*, 100.

47. Lyttelton, "Building the Italian Nation." See also P. Del Negro, *Esercito, Stato, Society* (Bologna, 1979), 169–261; John Gooch, *Army, State, and Society in Italy, 1870–1915* (New York: St. Martin's Press, 1989).

48. Duggan, *Concise History of Italy,* 137.

49. Clark, *Modern Italy,* 49–50.

50. Richard B. Morris, ed., *Encyclopedia of American History* (New York: Harper & Row, 1970), 149, 197–98.

51. Ernest Renan, "What Is a Nation?," 53.

52. Zelinsky, *Nation into State*, 126–43.

53. Quoted in Lipset, *The First New Nation*, 19 n. 6.

54. Zelinsky, *Nation into State*, 186.

55. Riall, "Hero, Saint or Revolutionary?," 198.

56. Porciani, *Festa della nazione*, 56, quoting an article in *Civilta' Cattolica*, 1897. See also Sergio Raffaelli, "I nomi delle vie," in Isnenghi, ed., *I luoghi della memoria,* 215–42.

57.Rafaelli, "I nomi delle vie"; Giovanna Massobrio, *L'Italia per Garibaldi* (Milan: SugarCo, 1982), is a large catalog of the numerous monuments to Garibaldi across Italy.

58. Mack Smith, *Italy and Its Monarchy,* 5–6, 72.

59. Dickie, *"La macchina da scrivere,"* 261–85; Tobia, *L'Altare della patria.*

60. L'Enfant to George Washington, September 11, 1789, American Treasures of the Library of Congress, <http://www.loc.gov/exhibits/treasures/tri001.html>.

4. IMAGINED ENEMIES

1. Potter, *Impending Crisis,* 476.

2. Mack Smith, *Making of Italy,* 364.

3. Abba, *Diary of One of Garibaldi's Thousand*, 7.

4. Ibid., 54–55.

5. Gabriella Gribaudi, "Images of the South: The *Mezzogiorno* as seen by Insiders and Outsiders," in Lumley and Morris, eds., *New History of the Italian South*, 83–113, esp. 89.

6. Paolo Solaroli, quoted in Nelson Moe, "'Altro che Italia!' Il Sud die Piemontesi (1860–61)," *Meridiana* 15 (1992): 68. This fine essay is now available in English as "'This Is Africa': Ruling and Representing Southern Italy, 1860–61," in Ascoli and Henneberg, eds., *Making and Remaking Italy*, 119–54.

7. Farini to Minghetti, Naples, December 12, 1860, quoted in Mack Smith, *Making of Italy*, 330–31.

8. Farini to Cavour, October 27, 1860, quoted in Dickie, *Darkest Italy*, 35.

9. Bianco di Saint Jorioz, *Il brigantaggio alla frontiera pontificia, 1860–63* (Milan: Daelli, 1864), 391, quoted in Dickie, *Darkest Italy*, 36.

10. Moe, "'Altro che Italia!,'" 63.

11. Ibid., 67.

12. Ibid., 72.

13. Dickie, *Darkest Italy*, 36.

14. P. Cala' Ulloa, *Lettres Napolitaines* (Paris, 1864), 87–92, quoted in Mack Smith, *Making of Italy*, 369.

15. Massimo d'Azeglio to C. Matteucci, August 2, 1861, quoted in Mack Smith, *Making of Italy*, 367.

16. Horace Bushnell, *A Discourse on the Slavery Question: Delivered in the North Church, Hartford, January 10, 1839* (Hartford, Conn.: N.p., 1839), 6, 15, quoted in Susan-Mary Grant, *North over South*, 48; Don H. Doyle, "Slavery, Secession, and Reconstruction as American Problems," in *The South as an American Problem*, ed. Griffin and Doyle, 102–25.

17. Grant, *North over South*, 58, 73; Renan, "What Is a Nation?," 45. Grant is exploring the historical background to what Eric Foner describes as the Republican Party's "critique of the South"; see Foner, *Free Soil, Free Labor, Free Men*, 40–72.

18. Foner, *Free Soil, Free Labor, Free Men*; Grant, *North over South*; Leonard L. Richards, *The Slave Power: The Free North and Southern*

Domination, 1780–1860 (Baton Rouge: Louisiana State University Press, 2001).

19. <http://www.tncrimlaw.com/civil_bible/house_divided.htm>.

20. Russell B. Nye, "The Slave Power Conspiracy, 1830–1860," *Science and Society* 10 (Summer 1946): 262–74; Potter, *Impending Crisis*, 349.

21. *Oxford Observer,* July 13, 1844; Bradley G. Bond, *Political Culture in the Nineteenth-Century South: Mississippi, 1830–1900* (Baton Rouge: Louisiana State University Press, 1995), 95. See also Huff, "Eagle and the Vulture."

22. James B. Murphy, *L. Q. C. Lamar: Pragmatic Patriot* (Baton Rouge: Louisiana State University Press, 1973), 38.

23. Ibid., 49.

24. McPherson, *Is Blood Thicker than Water?*, 45; Grant, *North over South*, 54, 58; William R. Taylor, *Cavalier and Yankee: The Old South and American National Character* (New York: G. Braziller, 1961).

25. Faust, *Creation of Confederate Nationalism,* 9–13.

26. Grant, *North over South*, [vii].

27. *Journal of the State Convention* (Jackson, Miss.: E. Barksdale, State Printer, 1861), 86–88.

28. For all the Confederate secession ordinances, see <http://www.dixienet.org/csa-docs/ordinanc.html>.

29. From his "Cornerstone Speech," reprinted in Henry Cleveland, *Alexander H. Stephens, in Public and Private: With Letters and Speeches, before, during, and since the War* (Philadelphia, 1886), 717–29, reproduced at <http://members.aol.com/jfepperson/corner.html>.

30. Reverend John H. Aughey, *The Iron Furnace: or, Slavery and Secession* (Philadelphia: William S. and Alfred Martien, 1863), 51–52.

31. Potter, *Impending Crisis*, 478.

32. Faust, *Creation of Confederate Nationalism*, 14; Beringer, Hattaway, Jones, and Still, *Elements of Confederate Defeat*, 30.

33. Potter, *Impending Crisis*, 469.

34. Ibid., 471, n. 49.

35. Greenfeld, *Nationalism*, 15–17, 177–84.

36. Elson, *Guardians of Tradition*, 180, 329.

37. Accounts of this event are taken from *Mercury* (Oxford), March 9,

106 Notes

1861, reprinted in *Lamar Rifles: A History of Company G, Eleventh Mississippi Regiment, C.S.A.* (1901; rpt. Topeka, Kans.: Bonnie Blue Press, 1992), 52–57; *Oxford Intelligencer*, March 20, 1861. Transcripts of the speech differ slightly in the two accounts.

38. Drew Gilpin Faust, *Mothers of Invention: Women of the Slaveholding South in the American Civil War* (Chapel Hill: University of North Carolina Press, 1996). See also Frank Lawrence Owsley, *State Rights in the Confederacy* (1925; rpt. Gloucester, Mass.: Peter Smith, 1961).

39. Gary Gallagher, *The Confederate War* (Cambridge, Mass.: Harvard University Press, 1997).

40. Murrin, "Roof without Walls," 344–45.

41. Faust, *Creation of Confederate Nationalism*, 6.

42. Potter, "The Historian's Uses of Nationalism and Vice Versa," 88.

43. Renan, "What Is a Nation?," 53.

44. *Proceedings of the Tenth Annual Convention of the Texas Division of the United Daughters of the Confederacy . . . 1905* (Weatherford, Tex.: Herald, 1906), 50; Cornelia Branch Stone, "U. D. C. Catechism for Children," Galveston UDC Records, both quoted in Elizabeth Hayes Turner, *Women, Culture, and Community: Religion and Reform in Galveston, 1880–1920* (New York: Oxford University Press, 1997), 174–75.

45. Hobsbawm, *Nations and Nationalism since 1780*, 12.

46. David W. Blight, *Race and Reunion: The Civil War in American Memory* (Cambridge, Mass.: Harvard University Press, 2001), 4.

47. Renan, "What Is a Nation," 45, 49.

48. Dickie, *Darkest Italy*; Claudia Petraccone, *Le due civiltà: settentrionali e meridionali nella storia d'Italia* (Rome: Laterza, 2000).

49. Levy, ed., *Italian Regionalism*, provides a good overview of the history of regionalism in Italy. "Extra-communitarian" refers to those outside the European Community but usually refers to those from Africa, the Middle East, and Eastern Europe.

5. NATIONALISM RECONSIDERED

1. Ernesto Galli Della Loggia, *La morte della patria: la crisi dell'idea di nazione tra resistenza, antifascismo e repubblica* (Rome: Laterza, 1996);

Aldo Schiavone, *Italiani senza Italia: storia e identità* (Turin: Einaudi, 1998); Fondazione "Amici di *Liberal*," ed., *Risorgimento imperfetto: perché da Cavour siamo arrivati a Bossi* (Rome: Liberal, [1997]). See also Della Loggia, *L'identità italiana* (Bologna: Mulino, 1998).

2. Wiebe, "Humanizing Nationalism," distinguishes between nationalism and the horrible things states do in its name. Students of nationalism await his forthcoming book, published posthumously, *Who We Are: A History of Popular Nationalism* (Princeton: Princeton University Press, 2002).

3. Mack Smith, *Mazzini,* 11–12, 52, 220–21.

4. Timothy Garton Ash, "Joining the Continent to Unite the Kingdom," *New York Times*, June 17, 2001. I thank Ed Harcourt for bringing this article to my attention.

5. See the English version of the Northern League's web site: <http://www.leganord.org/frames/english.htm>.

6. John Dickie, "Fantasy Maps," in Forgacs and Lumley, eds., *Italian Cultural Studies,* 102–4.

7. Abraham Lincoln, "First Inaugural Address," March 4, 1861, in Roy P. Basler and Christian O. Basler, eds., *Collected Works of Abraham Lincoln,* 8 vols. (New Brunswick: Rutgers University Press, 1953), 4:269; available in electronic form at <http://www.hti.umich.edu/l/lincoln/>.

BIBLIOGRAPHY

NATIONALISM, GENERAL STUDIES

Alter, Peter. *Nationalism.* 2d ed. London: Peter Arnold, 1994.

Anderson, Benedict. *Imagined Communities: Reflections on the Origin and Spread of Nationalism.* 2d ed. New York: Verso, 1991.

Armstrong, John A. *Nations before Nationalism.* Chapel Hill: University of North Carolina Press, 1982.

Breuilly, John. *Nationalism and the State.* 2d ed. Chicago: University of Chicago Press, 1985.

Buchanan, Allen. *Secession: The Morality of Political Divorce from Fort Sumter to Lithuania and Quebec.* Boulder: Westview Press, 1991.

Colley, Linda. *Britons: Forging the Nation, 1707–1837.* New Haven: Yale University Press, 1992.

Davis, David Brion. *Revolutions: Reflections on American Equality and Foreign Liberations.* Cambridge, Mass.: Harvard University Press, 1990.

Eley, Geoff, and Ronald Grigor Suny, eds. *Becoming National: A Reader.* New York: Oxford University Press, 1996.

Fredrickson, George M. *The Comparative Imagination: On the History of Racism, Nationalism, and Social Movements.* Berkeley: University of California Press, 1997.

Gellner, Ernest. *Encounters with Nationalism.* Cambridge, Mass.: Blackwell, 1994.

———. *Nations and Nationalism.* Ithaca: Cornell University Press, 1983.

Gillis, John R., ed. *Commemorations: The Politics of National Identity.* Princeton: Princeton University Press, 1994.

Greenfeld, Liah. *Nationalism: Five Roads to Modernity.* Cambridge, Mass.: Harvard University Press, 1992.

Hastings, Adrian. *The Construction of Nationhood: Ethnicity, Religion and Nationalism.* Cambridge, Eng.: Cambridge University Press, 1998.

Hobsbawm, E. J. *Nations and Nationalism since 1780: Programme, Myth, Reality.* New York: Cambridge University Press, 1990.

Hobsbawm, Eric, and Terence Ranger, eds. *The Invention of Tradition.* New York: Cambridge University Press, 1983.

Hutchinson, John, and Anthony D. Smith. *Nationalism: Critical Concepts in Political Science.* Rev. ed. New York: Routledge, 2000.

Ignatieff, Michael. *Blood and Belonging: Journeys into the New Nationalism.* New York: Farrar, Straus, and Giroux, 1994.

Kennedy, Paul M. "The Decline of Nationalistic History in the West, 1900–1970." *Journal of Contemporary History* 8 (1973): 77–100.

Lehning, Percy B., ed. *Theories of Secession.* European Political Science Series. London: Routledge, 1998.

McPherson, James M. *Is Blood Thicker than Water? Crises of Nationalism in the Modern World.* New York: Vintage, 1998.

Moore, Margaret, ed. *National Self-Determination and Secession.* New York: Oxford University Press, 1998.

Mortimer, Edward, ed. *People, Nation, and State: The Meaning of Ethnicity and Nationalism.* London: I. B. Tauris, 1999.

Mosse, George L. *The Nationalization of the Masses: Political Symbolism and Mass Movements in Germany from the Napoleonic Wars through the Third Reich.* New York: H. Fertig, 1975.

Nairn, Tom. *The Faces of Nationalism: Janus Revisited.* New York: Verso, 1997.

Schwartz, Bryan. *Last Best Hope: Quebec Secession—Lincoln's Lessons for Canada.* Calgary, Alberta: Detselig Enterprises, 1998.

Shreeves, W. G. *Nationmaking in Nineteenth Century Europe: The National Unification of Italy and Germany, 1815–1914.* Nelson Advanced Studies in History. Walton-on-Thames, U.K.: Nelson, 1984.

Smith, Anthony D. *Nationalism and Modernism: A Critical Survey of Recent Theories of Nations and Nationalism.* London: Routledge, 1998.

————. *Nationalist Movements.* New York: St. Martin's Press, 1977.

Suny, Ronald Grigor. "Constructing Primordialism: Old Histories for New Nations." *Journal of Modern History,* forthcoming.

Tyrell, Ian. "American Exceptionalism in an Age of International History." *American Historical Review* 96 (1991): 1031–55.

Viroli, Maruizio. *For Love of Country: An Essay on Patriotism and Nationalism.* New York: Oxford University Press, 1995.

Weber, Eugen. *Peasants into Frenchmen: The Modernization of Rural France, 1870–1914.* Stanford: Stanford University Press, 1976.

Wiebe, Robert H. "Humanizing Nationalism." *World Policy Journal* 13 (Winter 1996–97): 81–88.

————. "Imagined Communities, Nationalist Experiences." *Journal of the Historical Society* 1 (Spring 2000): 33–63.

————. *Who We Are: A History of Popular Nationalism.* Princeton: Princeton University Press, 2002.

THE UNITED STATES

Albanese, Catherine L. *Sons of the Fathers: The Civil Religion of the American Revolution.* Philadelphia: Temple University Press, 1976.

Appleby, Joyce Oldham. *Inheriting the Revolution: The First Generation of Americans.* Cambridge, Mass.: Belknap Press of Harvard University Press, 2000.

Arieli, Yehoshua. "Nationalism." In *Encyclopedia of American Political History: Studies of the Principal Movements and Ideas,* edited by Jack P. Greene. 3 vols. New York: Scribner, 1984. 2:841–62.

Beeman, Richard, Stephen Botein, and Edward C. Carter II, eds. *Beyond Confederation: Origins of the Constitution and American National Identity.* Chapel Hill: University of North Carolina Press, 1987.

Bensel, Richard Franklin. *Yankee Leviathan: The Origins of Central State Authority in America, 1859–1877.* New York: Cambridge University Press, 1990.

Beringer, Richard E., Herman Hattaway, Archer Jones, and William N. Still Jr. *The Elements of Confederate Defeat: Nationalism, War Aims, and Religion.* Athens: University of Georgia Press, 1988.

Bodnar, John E., ed. *Bonds of Affection: Americans Define Their Patriotism*. Princeton: Princeton University Press, 1996.

Breen, T. H. "Ideology and Nationalism on the Eve of the American Revolution: Revisions Once More in Need of Revising." *Journal of American History* 84 (1997): 13–39.

Carpenter, Charles H. *History of American Schoolbooks*. Philadelphia: University of Pennsylvania Press, 1963.

Channing, Stephen A. "Slavery and Confederate Nationalism." In *From the Old South to the New: Essays on the Transitional South*, edited by Walter J. Fraser and Winifred B. Moore. Westport, Conn.: Greenwood, 1981.

Commager, Henry Steele. "The Origins and Nature of American Nationalism." In *Jefferson, Nationalism, and the Enlightenment*. New York: Braziller, 1975.

Craven, Avery. *The Growth of Southern Nationalism, 1848–1861*. Baton Rouge: Louisiana State University Press, 1953.

Curti, Merle. *The Roots of American Loyalty*. New York: Columbia University Press, 1946.

Elson, Ruth Miller. *Guardians of Tradition: American Textbooks of the Nineteenth Century*. Lincoln: University of Nebraska Press, 1964.

Faust, Drew Gilpin. *The Creation of Confederate Nationalism: Ideology and Identity in the Civil War South*. Baton Rouge: Louisiana State University Press, 1988.

FitzGerald, Frances. *America Revised: History Schoolbooks in the Twentieth Century*. Boston: Little, Brown, 1979.

Floan, Howard Russell. *The South in Northern Eyes, 1831 to 1861*. New York: McGraw-Hill, 1958.

Foner, Eric. *Free Soil, Free Labor, Free Men: The Ideology of the Republican Party before the Civil War*. New York: Oxford University Press, 1970.

Foster, Gaines M. *Ghosts of the Confederacy: Defeat, the Lost Cause, and the Emergence of the New South*. New York: Oxford University Press, 1987.

Gerstle, Gary. "Liberty, Coercion, and the Making of Americans." *Journal of American History* 84 (September 1997): 524–58.

Grant, Susan-Mary. *North over South: Northern Nationalism and American Identity in the Antebellum Era*. Lawrence: University Press of Kansas, 2000.

Green, Fletcher M. "Listen to the Eagle Scream: One Hundred Years of the Fourth of July in North Carolina, 1776–1876." In *Democracy in the Old South, and Other Essays by Fletcher Melvin Green*, edited by J. Isaac Copeland, 111–56. Nashville: Vanderbilt University Press, 1969.

Greene, Jack P. *The Intellectual Construction of America: Exceptionalism and Identity from 1492 to 1800*. Chapel Hill: University of North Carolina Press, 1993.

Griffin, Larry, and Don H. Doyle, eds. *The South as an American Problem*. Athens: University of Georgia Press, 1995.

Gruver, Rebecca Brooks, comp. *American Nationalism, 1783–1830: A Self-Portrait*. New York: Putnam, 1970.

Hall, John A. *Is America Breaking Apart?* Princeton: Princeton University Press, 1999.

Hay, Robert Pettus. "Freedom's Jubilee: One Hundred Years of the Fourth of July, 1776–1876." Ph.D. diss., University of Kentucky, 1967.

Hays, Carlton J. H. *Nationalism: A Religion*. New York: Macmillan, 1960.

Hollinger, David A. "National Solidarity at the End of the Twentieth Century: Reflections on the United States and Liberal Nationalism." *Journal of American History* 84 (September 1997): 559–69.

Huff, A. V., Jr. "The Eagle and the Vulture: Changing Attitudes toward Nationalism in Fourth of July Orations Delivered in Charleston, 1778–1860." *South Atlantic Quarterly* 73 (1974): 10–22.

Kammen, Michael G. *A Season of Youth: The American Revolution and the Historical Imagination*. New York: Knopf, 1978.

Krakau, Knud, ed. *The American Nation, National Identity, Nationalism*. Studies in North American History, vol. 1. Munich: Lit Verlag, 1997.

Lipset, Seymour Martin. *American Exceptionalism: A Double-Edged Sword*. New York: Norton, 1996.

———. *The First New Nation: The United States in Historical and Comparative Perspective*. New York: Basic Books, 1963.

Loveland, Anne C. *Emblem of Liberty: The Image of Lafayette in the*

American Mind. Baton Rouge, Louisiana State University Press, 1971.

McCardell, John. *The Idea of a Southern Nation: Southern Nationalists and Southern Nationalism, 1830–1860.* New York: Norton, 1979.

Mathews, Donald G. "The Abolitionists on Slavery: The Critique behind the Social Movement." *Journal of Southern History* 33 (May 1967): 163–82.

Morris, Richard B. *The Emerging Nations and the American Revolution.* New York: Harper & Row, 1970.

Mulford, Elisha. *The Nation: The Foundations of Civil Order and Political Life in the United States.* New York: Hurd and Houghton, 1870.

Murrin, John M. "A Roof without Walls: The Dilemma of American National Identity." In *Beyond Confederation*, edited by Beeman, Botein, and Carter.

Myers, Robert J. *Celebrations: The Complete Book of American Holidays.* Garden City, N.Y.: Doubleday, 1972.

Nagel, Paul C. *One Nation Indivisible: The Union in American Thought, 1776–1861.* New York: Oxford University Press, 1964.

———. *This Sacred Trust: American Nationality, 1798–1898.* New York: Oxford University Press, 1971.

O'Leary, Cecilia Elizabeth. *To Die For: The Paradox of American Patriotism.* Princeton: Princeton University Press, 1999.

Palmer, Robert R. "The Impact of the American Revolution Abroad." In *The Impact of the American Revolution Abroad*, 5–19. Washington, D.C.: Library of Congress, 1976.

Pierce, Bessie Louise. *Civic Attitudes in American School Textbooks.* Chicago: University of Chicago Press, 1930.

Potter, David M. "The Historian's Use of Nationalism and Vice Versa." *American Historical Review* 67 (1962): 924–950. Also in Don E. Fehrenbacher, *History and American Society: Essays of David M. Potter.* London: Oxford University Press, 1973.

———. *The Impending Crisis, 1848–1861.* New York: Harper Torchbooks, 1976.

Reed, John Shelton. *The Enduring South: Subcultural Persistence in Mass Society.* Lexington, Mass: Lexington Books, 1972.

Rossiter, Clinton. *The American Quest, 1790–1860: An Emerging Nation in Search of Identity, Unity and Modernity.* New York: Harcourt Brace Jovanovich, 1971.

Snay, Mitchell. *Gospel of Disunion: Religion and Separatism in the Antebellum South.* Cambridge, Eng.: Cambridge University Press, 1993.

Somkin, Fred. *Unquiet Eagle: Memory and Desire in the Idea of American Freedom, 1815–1860.* Ithaca: Cornell University Press, 1967.

Spillman, Lynette P. *Nation and Commemoration: Creating National Identities in the United States and Australia.* New York: Cambridge University Press, 1997.

Travers, Len. *Celebrating the Fourth: Independence Day and the Rites of Nationalism in the Early Republic.* Amherst: University of Massachusetts Press, 1997.

Van Alstyne, Richard W. *Genesis of American Nationalism.* Waltham, Mass: Blaisdell, 1970.

Waldstreicher, David. *In the Midst of Perpetual Fetes: The Making of American Nationalism, 1776–1820.* Chapel Hill: University of North Carolina Press, 1997.

Wilson, Charles Reagan. *Baptized in Blood: The Religion of the Lost Cause, 1865–1920.* Athens: University of Georgia Press, 1980.

Wood, Gordon S. *The Creation of the American Republic, 1776–1787.* Chapel Hill: University of North Carolina Press, 1969.

Zelinsky, Wilbur. *Nation into State: The Shifting Symbolic Foundations of American Nationalism.* Chapel Hill: University of North Carolina Press, 1988.

ITALY

Abba, Giuseppe Cesare. *The Diary of One of Garibaldi's Thousand.* Translated by E. R. Vincent. London: Oxford University Press, 1962.

Alberti, Giovanni. *La non-nazione: Risorgimento e Italia unità tra storia e politica.* Pisa: Istituti editoriali, 1997.

Allen, Beverly, and Mary Russo, eds. *Revisioning Italy: National Identity and Global Culture.* Minneapolis: University of Minnesota Press, 1997.

Ascoli, Albert Russell, and Krystyna Von Henneberg, eds. *Making and Remaking Italy: The Cultivation of National Identity around the Risorgimento*. Oxford: Berg, 2001.

Baioni, Massimo. *La "religione della patria": musei e istituti del culto risorgimentale, 1884–1918*. Quinto di Treviso: Pagus, 1994.

Banti, Alberto M. *La nazione del Risorgimento: parentela, santità e onore alle origini dell'Italia unità*. Turin: Einaudi, 2000.

Beales, Derek. *The Risorgimento and the Unification of Italy*. London: Longman, 1981.

Bellocchi, Ugo. *Il tricolore: due cento anni, 1797–1997*. Modena: Articoli, 1996.

Bellosi, Giuseppe. *L'Altra lingua: letteraturea dialettale e folklore orale in Italia con profilo di storia linguistica*. Ravenna: Longo, 1980.

Bennett, C. W. *National Education: Italy, France, Germany, England and Wales, Popularly Considered*. American Library of Education, vol. 7. Syracuse, N.Y.: N.p., 1878.

Bevilacqua, Piero. *Breve storia dell'Italia meridionale dall'ottocento a oggi*. Rome: Donzelli, 1993.

Bogna, Ernesto. *Stato e scuola: materiali per una storia della scuola italiana*. Bari: Cacucci, 1998.

Bollati, Giulio. *L'Italiano: il carattere nazionale come storia e come invenzione*. Turin: Einaudi, 1983.

Brendon, Vyvyen. *The Making of Modern Italy, 1800–71*. London: Hodder and Stoughton, 1998.

Broccoli, Angelo. *Educazione e politica nel mezzogiorno d'Italia, 1767–1860*. Florence: La Nuova Italia, 1968.

Bruni, Francesco, ed. *L'Italiano nelle regioni, lingua nazionale e identità*. Turin: UTET, 1992.

Buffalino, Nicolas. "Giuseppe Garibaldi and Liberal Italy: History, Politics and Nostalgia, 1861–1915." Ph.D. diss., University of California, Berkeley, 1991.

Calabrese, Omar, et al., eds. *Modern Italy: Images and History of a National Identity*. Vol. 1, *From Unification to the New Century*. Milan: Electa, 1982. [also in Italian]

Candeloro, Giorgio. *Storia dell'Italia moderna.* Vols. 5 and 6. Milan: Feltrinelli, 1956–86.

Chabod, Federico. *L'Idea di nazione.* 1961. Reprint. Rome: Laterza 1997.

———. *Italian Foreign Policy: The Statecraft of the Founders.* Translated by William McCuaig and Giovanni Agnelli. Foundation Series in Italian History. 1951. Reprint. Princeton: Princeton University Press, 1996.

Comune di Milano. *Il mito del Risorgimento nell'italian unità.* Milan: Comune di Milano, 1995.

Confino, Alon. Review essay, "Making Italians: School and Culture in Modern Italy." *Social History* 22 (May 1997): 194–201.

Consulo, Ronald S. *Italian Nationalism: From Its Origins to World War II.* Malabar, Fla.: Robert E. Krieger, 1990.

———. "Italian Nationalism in Historical Perspective." *History of European Ideas* 16 (1993): 759–66.

Corgnati, Martina, G. Mullini, and F. Poli, eds. *Il lauro e il bronzo: la scultura celebrativa in Italia, 1800–1900.* Turin: Editris, 1990.

Croce, Benedetto. *A History of Italy, 1871–1915.* Translated by Cecilia M. Ady. Oxford: Clarendon Press, 1929.

Dardano, Maurizio. *Sparliamo Italiano: storia, costume, mode, virtu e peccati della nostra lingua.* Rome: A. Curcio, 1978.

Davis, John A. *Conflict and Control: Law and Order in Nineteenth-Century Italy.* London: Macmillan, 1988.

———, ed. *Gramsci and Italy's Passive Revolution.* London: Croom Helm, 1979.

Davis, John A., and Paul Ginsborg, eds. *Society and Politics in the Age of the Risorgimento: Essays in Honour of Denis Mack Smith.* Cambridge, Eng.: Cambridge University Press, 1991.

D'Azeglio, Massimo. *Things I Remember.* Translated and introduction by E. R. Vincent. Oxford: Oxford University Press, 1966.

De Amicis, Edmondo. *Cuore: The Heart of a Boy.* Translated by Desmond Hartley. 1886. Reprint. London: Peter Owen, 1986.

De Cesare, Giuseppe. *La formazione dello stato unitario (1860–1871).* Milan: Giuffre, 1978.

De Fort, Ester. *Storia della scuola elementare in Italia.* Vol. 1, *Dall unità all età Giolittiana.* Milan: Feltrinelli, 1979.

De Mauro, Tullio. *Storia linguistica del l'Italia unità.* Rome: Laterza, 1991.

DeVoto, Giacomo. *La lingua italiana: storia e problemi attuali.* 2d ed. Turin: ERI, 1979.

Dickie, John. *Darkest Italy: The Nation and Stereotypes of the Mezzogiorno, 1860–1900.* New York: St. Martin's Press, 1999.

———. "Imagined Italies." In David Forgacs and Robert Lumley, eds., *Italian Cultural Studies: An Introduction.* Oxford: Oxford University Press, 1996.

———. "La Macchina da Scrivere: The Victor Emmanuel Monument and Italian Nationalism." *Italianist* 14 (1994): 261–85.

———. "The South as Other: From Liberal Italy to the Lega Nord." In *Culture and Society in Southern Italy: Past and Present*, edited by Anna Cento Bull and A. Giorgio. Supplement to the *Italianist* 14 (1994): 124–40.

Drake, Richard. "The Theory and Practice of Italian Nationalism, 1900–1906." *Modern History* 53 (1981): 213–41.

Duggan, Christopher. *A Concise History of Italy.* Cambridge, Eng.: Cambridge University Press, 1994.

L'educazione civica nella scuola italiana: storia, problemi, e metodi. Rome: AIMC, 1970.

Fissore, Gianpaolo, and Giancarlo Meinardi, eds. *La questione meridionale.* Turin: Loescher, 1976.

Forgacs, David, and Robert Lumley, eds. *Italian Cultural Studies: An Introduction.* New York: Oxford University Press, 1996.

Gaeta, Franco. *Il nazionalismo italiano.* Rome: Laterza, 1981.

Gavelli, Mirtide, Otello Sangiori, and Fiorenza Tarozzi, eds. *Colorare la patria: tricolore e formazione della coscienza nazionale, 1797–1914.* Florence: Vallecchi, 1996.

Gooch, John. *Army, State, and Society in Italy, 1870–1915.* New York: St. Martin's Press, 1989.

Grew, Raymond. *A Sterner Plan for Italian Unity: The Italian National*

Society in the Risorgimento. Princeton: Princeton University Press, 1963.

Gribaudi, Gabriella. *A Eboli: il mondo meridionale in cent'anni di trasformazioni.* Venice: Marsilio, 1990.

Haupt, Heinz-Gerhard, Michael G. Muller, and Stuart Woolf, eds. *Regional and National Identities in Europe in the XIXth and XXth Centuries.* The Hague: Kluwer Law International, 1998.

Hearder, Harry. *Italy in the Age of the Risorgimento, 1790–1870.* London: Longman, 1983.

Hibbert, Christopher. *Garibaldi and His Enemies: The Clash of Arms and Personalities in the Making of Italy.* 1965. Reprint. London: Penguin, 1987.

Hobsbawm, E. J. *Primitive Rebels: Studies in the Archaic Forms of Social Movements in the 19th and 20th Centuries.* Manchester: Manchester University Press, 1959.

Hughes, H. Stuart. *The U.S. and Italy.* 3d ed. Cambridge, Mass: Harvard University Press, 1980.

Isnenghi, Mario, ed. *I luoghi della memoria: personaggi e date dell'Italia unità.* Rome: Laterza, 1997.

———. *L'Italia in piazza: i luoghi della vita pubblica dal 1848 ai giorni nostri.* Milan: Mondadori, 1994.

Lanaro, Silvio. "Da contadini a italiani." In *Storia dell'agricoltura Italiana in età contemporanea,* edited by Piero Bevilacqua. Vol. 3, *Mercati e istitutzioni.* Venice: Marsilio, 1991.

———. "Dove comincia la nazione?" *Meridiana* nos. 11–12 (1991): 355.

———. *L'Italia nuova: identità e sviluppo, 1861–1988.* Turin: Einaudi, 1988.

———. *Nazione e lavoro: Saggio sulla cultura borghese in Italia* (1870–1925). Venice: Marsilio, 1979.

Levra, Umberto. *Fare gli Italiani: memoria e celebrazione del Risorgimento.* Turin: Comitato di Torino dell'Istituto per la Storia del Risorgimento Italiano, 1992.

Levy, Carl, ed. *Italian Regionalism: History, Identity and Politics.* Washington, D.C.: Berg, 1996.

Lumley, Robert, and Jonathan Morris, eds. *The New History of the Italian South: The Mezzogiorno Revisted.* Exeter: University of Exeter Press, 1997.

Lupo, Salvatore. *Storia della Mafia dalle origine ai giorni nostri.* Rome: Donezelli, 1993.

Lyttleton, Adrian. "The National Question in Italy." In Mikulas Teich and Roy Porter, *The National Question in Europe in Historical Context,* 63–105. Cambridge, Eng.: Cambridge University Press, 1993.

Mack Smith, Denis. *Garibaldi: A Great Life in Brief.* New York: Knopf, 1956. Reprint.

———, ed. *Garibaldi.* Great Lives Observed. Englewood Cliffs, N.J.: Prentice-Hall, 1969.

———. *Italy and Its Monarchy.* New Haven: Yale University Press, 1989.

———. *Italy: A Modern History.* Ann Arbor: University of Michigan Press, 1969.

———. *The Making of Italy, 1796–1870.* New York: Walker, 1968.

———. *Mazzini.* New Haven: Yale University Press, 1994.

———. *Victor Emmanuel, Cavour, and the Risorgimento.* New York: Oxford University Press, 1971.

Macry, Paolo. *Ottocento: famiglia, elites e patrimoni a Napoli.* Turin: Einaudi, 1988.

———. "La questione scolastica: Controllo, conscenza, consenso (1860–1872)." *Quaderni Storici* 15 (1980): 867–93.

Manzoni, Alessandro. *The Betrothed.* Translated by David Forgacs. London: Dent, 1997.

Marraro, Howard R. *American Opinion on the Unification of Italy, 1846–1861.* Italian History Society Edition. New York: Columbia University Press, 1932.

Molfese, Franco. *Storia del brigantaggio dopo l'Unità.* Milan: Feltrinelli, 1979.

Nasto, Luciano. *Le feste civili a Roma nell'ottocento.* Rome: Gruppo editoriale, 1994.

Nitti, F. S. *Scritti sulla questione meridionale.* Bari: 1958.

Pagella, Mario. *Storia della scuola.* Bologna: Cappelli, 1980.

Patriarca, Silvano. *Numbers and Nationhood: Writing Statistics in Nineteenth-Century Italy.* Cambridge, Eng.: Cambridge University Press, 1996.

Perfetti, Francesco. *Il nazionalismo italiano dalle origini alla fusione col fascismo.* Bologna: Cappelli, 1977.

Petrusewicz, Marta. *Come il meridione divenne una questione: rappresentazione del Sud prima e dopo il quarantotto.* Soveria Mannelli (Catanzaro): Rubbettino, 1998.

————. *Latifundium: Moral Economy and Material Life in a European Periphery.* Translated by Judith C. Green. Ann Arbor: University of Michigan Press, 1996.

Pezzino, Paolo. *Il paradiso abitato da diavoli: società, elites, istitutionzi nel Mezzogiorno contemporaneo.* Milan: Angeli, 1992.

Porciani, Ilaria. *La Festa della Nazione: Rappresentazione dello Stato e Spazi Sociale nell'Italia Unità.* Bologna: Mulino, 1997.

Putnam, Robert D., et al. *Making Democracy Work: Civic Traditions in Modern Italy.* Princeton: Princeton University Press, 1993.

Ragazzini, Dario. *Storia della scuola italiana: linee generali e problemi divicerca.* Florence: Le Mannier, 1983.

Riall, Lucy. "Hero, Saint, or Revolutionary? Nineteenth-Century Politics and the Cult of Garibaldi." *Modern Italy* 3 (1998): 191–204.

————. *The Italian Risorgimento: State, Society, and National Unification.* London: Routledge, 1994.

————. *Sicily and the Unification of Italy: Liberal Policy and Local Power, 1859–1866.* Oxford: Clarendon Press, 1998.

Ricuperati, Giuseppe. "L'insegnamento della storia dall'età della sinistra ad oggi." *Società e Storia* 6 (1979): 763–92.

Ridley, Jasper. *Garibaldi.* London: Constable, 1974.

Romanelli, R. *Il commando impossibilie: state e società nell'Italia liberale.* Bologna: Mulino, 1988.

————. *L'Italia liberale.* Bologna: Mulino, 1990.

Romeo, Rosario. *Mezzogiorno e Sicilia nel Risorgimento.* Naples: ESI, 1963.

Rosati, Massimo. *Il patriotismo italiano.* Rome: Laterza, 2000.

Rugin, Santoni, et al. *Storia della scuola e storia d'Italia dall'unità ad oggi.* Bari: De Donato, 1982.

Sabbatuci, Giovanni, and Vittorio Vidotto, eds. *Il nuovo stato e la società civile, 1861–1887.* Vol. 2, *Storia d'Italia.* Rome: Laterza, 1995.

Salvadori, Massimo L. *Il mito del buongoverno: la questione meridonale da Cavour a Gramsci.* Turin: Einaudi, 1960.

Schneider, Jane, ed. *Italy's "Southern Question": Orientalism in One Country.* Oxford: Berg, 1998.

Seton-Watson, Christopher. *Italy from Liberalism to Fascism, 1870–1925.* London: Methuen, 1967.

Soldani, Simonetta, and Gabriele Turi, eds. *Fare gli Italiani: scuola e cultura nell'Italia contemporanea.* 2 vols. Vol. 1, *La nascita dello stato nazionale.* Bologna: Mulino, 1993.

Soldani, Simonetta. "Il Risorgimento a scuola: Incertezze dello stato e lenta formazione di un pubblico dei lettori." In *Alfredo Oriani e la cultura del suo tempo,* edited by Ennio Dirani, 133–72. Ravenna: Longo, 1985.

Spadolini, Giovani, ed. *Nazione e nazionalità in Italia: dall'alba del decolo ai nostri giorni.* Rome: Laterza, 1994.

Tarozzi, Fiorenza, and Giorgio Vecchio, eds. *Gli Italiani e il tricolore: patriottismo, identità nazionale e fratture sociali lungo due secoli di storia.* Bologna: Mulino, 1999.

Tobia, Bruno. *L'Altare della Patria.* Bologna: Mulino, 1998.

———. "Una cultura per la nuova Italia." In *Il nuovo stato e la società civile, 1861–1887,* edited by Giovanni Sabbatuci and Vittorio Vidotto. Vol. 2, *Storia d'Italia.* Rome: Laterza, 1995.

———. *Una patria per gli Italiani: spazi, itinerare, monumenti nell'Italia unità (1870–1900).* Rome: Laterza, 1991.

———. "Urban Space and Monuments in the 'Nationalization of the Masses': The Italian Case" (1979). Translated by Kathy Wolf in *Nationalism in Europe, 1815 to the Present: A Reader,* edited by Stuart Woolf, 171–91. London: Routledge, 1996.

Trevelyan, George Macaulay. *Garibaldi and the Making of Italy.* New York: Longmans, Green, 1911.

Villari, Pasquale. *Le lettere meridionali ed altri scritti sulla questione sociale in Italia.* Introduction by Francesco Barbagallo. 1878. Reprint. Naples: Guida Editori, 1979.

Villari, Rosario, ed. *Il Sud nella storia d'Italia: antologia della questione meridionale*. Rome: Laterza, 1961.

Volpe, Gioacchino. *Italia moderna, 1815–1915*. Florence: Sansoni, 1973.

White, Steven F. *Progressive Renaissance: America and the Reconstruction of Italian Education, 1943–1962*. Modern European History: Italy. New York: Garland, 1991.

Whittam, John. *The Politics of the Italian Army, 1861–1918*. London: Croom Helm, 1976.

Woolf, Stuart. *A History of Italy, 1700–1860: The Social Constraints of Political Change*. 1979. Reprint. London: Routledge, 1991.

———, comp. *The Italian Risorgimento*. New York: Barnes & Noble, 1969.

INDEX

Pledge of Allegiance, 49, 53

postnational era, 8, 95

Potter, David, 83, 86

primordialism, 12, 13, 15, 20, 28, 79, 80, 88

Puritan-Cavalier thesis, 79, 80

Quebec, 6

race: and Civil War, 87–88; and southern nationalism, 81–82

Ranger, Terence, 12

Rattazzi, Urbano, 61

reconciliation, between North and South, 87

Reconstruction, 70

religion. *See* nationalism: and religion

Renaissance, 28

Renan, Ernest, 35, 58, 75, 87–88

Republic of Rome, 30

Republican Party, 76, 77, 80

resentment, 33–34, 83, 84, 88

Risorgimento, 27–28, 44, 60

Rome, 27–28, 30, 31

Russia, 7

Sacconi, Giuseppe, 63

Savoy, House of, 30, 46, 62

schools. *See* education

Scotland, 7

Scott, Walter, 79

secession, 65, 80, 94, 98 (n. 12). *See also* separatism

separate origins myth, 79, 80

separatism, 6–9, 65, 66, 78, 79, 86, 98 (n. 12). *See also* secession

September 20, 48

Sherman, William T., 69

Sicily, 30, 31, 68–70, 89

Slave Power, 76, 77

slavery, 23, 27, 80, 81, 83, 85, 87; as national problem, 74, 76–77; and sectional antagonism, 75;

Smith, Anthony D., xiii, 13

South. *See* Italian South; United States South

South America. *See* Latin America

southern nationalism, 36, 81–85; and American Revolution, 83; and race, 81

Southern Question, 5, 66, 73, 88

southern rights, 78

Soviet Union, 6

Spence, James, 9

Statuto Day, 44–47

Stendahl, 29

Stephens, Alexander, 81

Strong, George Templeton, 80

suffrage, 32, 54

Sumner, Charles, 11, 83

Suny, Ronald Grigor, xiii, 14

Switzerland, 29

temperance, 43–44

Tennessee Valley Authority, 89

terrone, 88, 94